KATHARINA
WEISS-TUIDER

Translated by SHELLEY TANAKA

Illustrated by
CHRISTIAN SCHNEIDER

MISSION: ARCTIC

A SCIENTIFIC ADVENTURE TO A CHANGING NORTH POLE

GREYSTONE KIDS
GREYSTONE BOOKS · VANCOUVER/BERKELEY/LONDON

PART 3

100 OUR ARCTIC, OUR FUTURE

FOREWORD:
FROZEN IN THE ICE

It's an amazing experience to stand on an Arctic ice floe in the middle of the polar night. That's when winter plunges the NORTH POLE into inky blackness for almost half a year. The world shrinks to the small circle of light thrown by your own headlamp. Only your high-tech polar gear prevents your nose, fingers, or other body parts from freezing in the icy wind, at what feels like -60°C (-76°F). Most of the time there is nothing around you but deep silence. Unless, of course, a storm whistles over the ice, making it hard to spot stalking polar bears. When that happens, all you can do is return to the ship. During our expedition to the North Pole, the research icebreaker POLARSTERN shone like a bright point on the horizon at night—the only place where we humans could survive in this icy world.

I love the Arctic, in spite of its dangers. There's a reason why polar explorers talk about being bitten by the polar "bug" that keeps you coming back to this icy world. Polar research remains a tremendous adventure to this day.

THE ARCTIC IS THE EPICENTER OF CLIMATE CHANGE.

But the Arctic is changing dramatically. Nowhere on Earth is climate change as clearly visible as it is here. I have been traveling north as a scientist since the early 1990s. When I came to the Arctic island of Svalbard during the winter about thirty years ago, I stepped into a deeply frozen landscape of blue ice blocks and glittering snow crystals. Anyone who wanted to cross the fjord to get to our research station did so on skis or snowmobiles, because the water in the narrow bay was frozen and lay before us as a massive sheet of ice.

When I come to the station these days, water splashes at my feet, even in winter. The fjord no longer freezes over. Instead of skiing over the ice, today we have to cross the fjord by boat.

But what happens in the Arctic does not stay in the Arctic. It has a direct impact on the weather and climate in the rest of the world. Yet the Arctic is the climatic region that we know the least about, because the thick ice, the cold, and the darkness of the polar night have always stopped science from uncovering its secrets.

EXPEDITION LEADER MARKUS REX IS A POLAR AND ATMOSPHERIC SCIENTIST.

That's why we set out on an unprecedented expedition in the fall of 2019. We let the *Polarstern* freeze in the sea ice and drift with the ice toward the North Pole, without knowing exactly where this journey might take us. Almost five hundred people from all over the world braved the ice, bears, and storms, as did a fleet of other icebreakers, ships, and helicopters that supported the expedition while we were in the ice.

Thanks to this largest ever expedition to the Arctic, we were able to explore the region around the North Pole like never before. We could observe the many small processes that make up the Arctic climate system. They are like cogs in a wheel, or like the small pieces of a puzzle, and we have to know each piece to understand how to put the big puzzle together.

That's what this book is all about. It will tell the story of the *Polarstern* expedition, whisk you away to an endlessly fascinating icy world, and show why this ice is not as permanent as we thought. It explains how the many individual parts in the climate system are connected, and why a lot of things that seem to happen so far away from us have much more to do with our weather than we realize.

We still have a few years to prevent some of the most dramatic changes in the Earth's climate system, such as stopping the north from becoming ice-free in summer. The knowledge that we bring home from the ice will help determine our future, and our children's future. It is this knowledge that can help us to protect "our" climate, as well as the Arctic ecosystem.

MARKUS REX, *EXPEDITION LEADER*
SEPTEMBER 2020, AT 89° NORTH, 109° EAST

THE BIGGEST ARCTIC EXPEDITION OF ALL TIME

OUR PLAN SOUNDS A BIT KOOKY. BUT CLIMATE CHANGE AFFECTS US ALL, AND ONLY OUT THERE ON THE ICE WILL WE FIND THE INFORMATION WE NEED TO UNDERSTAND IT. SO COME ALONG WITH US TO THE NORTH POLE!

The *Polarstern* is a very special ship—a research icebreaker. It has been on many expeditions over the past four decades, but none as big, as expensive, as long—or as daring—as this one.

Now the *Polarstern* is on its way to the Central Arctic, one of the most extreme regions on Earth. On board are a hundred people from all over the world—people of all ages and from a wide variety of professions, from researchers, logistics experts, and polar bear guards to captains and engineers, doctors, cooks, and navigators.

High above them shines the star that the ship is named after—Polaris, the North Star. It will show them the way to the Central Arctic, far up in the north. Only a few people have ever reached this area around the North Pole.

Humans have been on the moon and in the deepest depths of the oceans. People are living on a space station, and our space probes have gone past the limits of our solar system. We have already explored and discovered so much. But the Central Arctic is still a big mystery to us. The pack ice is so thick in winter that even icebreakers can't make it near the North Pole. The ice and cold and the darkness of the polar night block our way into this beautiful but inhospitable world of eternal ice.

THE PLAN

The *Polarstern* and her one hundred passengers will be frozen in the Arctic ice for one year. We can't navigate our way to the North Pole in the winter, but we can drift there with the sea ice and explore the Arctic while we're at it—in temperatures as cold as -45°C (-49°F) and in darkness that will last for months.

THIS IS STILL TRUE, BUT THE ICE IS NOT AS PERMANENT AS WE THOUGHT.

The Arctic is changing in dramatic ways, and the entire planet is changing along with it. Although we already know that these changes in the Arctic and their effects on the world's climate will be huge, we do not yet know the exact extent of these changes. We urgently need to understand better how human activity has and is affecting the climate.

So the *Polarstern* expedition is pursuing an important goal: to find out what's going on with climate change. The scientific data that the team collects can help people all over the world to take action against climate change and its consequences.

THE *POLARSTERN* IN SEPTEMBER 2019, MAKING HER WAY THROUGH THE ARCTIC OCEAN ON AN EXPEDITION UNLIKE ANY SHE HAS BEEN ON BEFORE.

THINGS ARE HEATING UP!

← CLIMATE CHANGE IS ALTERING THE PLANET.

Climate change affects us all, no matter how old we are or what we do for a living, how rich we are, whether we care about the climate and the Earth or not. However, some of us are struggling with the consequences of global warming more often and more quickly than others. It depends on where we live, because the effects are not the same all over the world.

Above all, climate change affects you! Today's kids will have to live with ever greater IMPACTS ON THE CLIMATE in the future. More and more young people are becoming aware of this and, fortunately, so are more and more adults. They are demanding that the world community finally do something against global warming and change the way we treat the Earth, because it is our home, and we need to take better care of it. People are now urging politicians and business leaders to take the scientific facts seriously and make sure that humans release fewer climate-damaging greenhouse gases into the atmosphere. And people are saying that these things must happen right now and not at some point down the road, when today's kids will be grown-ups themselves and having to live with the consequences of global warming.

Of course, not everyone wants to hear that people around the world need to be more committed to saving the planet. Some people even get irritated. Hardly anyone likes to hear that we are the ones causing climate change with our own unsustainable lifestyle.

Climate change also brings more EXTREME WEATHER, which is causing serious damage here and now, and will have big consequences down the road for people and nature.

People who deny climate change often claim that extreme weather has always existed!

WHICH IS TRUE, BUT THEY ARE OVERLOOKING SOMETHING.

Climate change does not cause extreme weather. However, climate change does mean that extreme weather events happen more often, and so the effects are getting worse. For example, droughts have always occurred. But when they occur more frequently, nature does not have a chance to recover as well between droughts. The soil dries out more and more, plants die of thirst, and forest fires occur more often. Harvests fail, and food becomes scarce. Animals die or have to leave the region. So the effects become more and more severe.

WHO WILL SAVE THE WORLD EXCEPT US?

THERE IS NO PLANET B

I CAN'T TIDY MY ROOM, I HAVE TO SAVE THE PLANET

RETTET DIE EISBÄREN

UNITED STATES, SUMMER 2005

Hurricane Katrina strikes the United States with one of the most devastating natural disasters in history. New Orleans is flooded by storm surges nearly 8 meters (26 feet) high. There is no electricity or drinking water. There is illness and death.

GERMANY AND THE CZECH REPUBLIC, SPRING 2006

An enormous flood inundates the region along the Elbe River.

GERMANY, AUGUST 2017

Storm Xavier arrives unusually early. The trees have not yet lost their leaves and offer the wind a good surface to attack. The gusts tear them down. Seven people die.

GERMANY, 2018

The warmest year on record! Extreme summer drought occurs throughout the country. Trees die, and the potato harvest shrinks by a quarter compared to the previous year.

AUSTRALIA, SUMMER 2019 TO WINTER 2020

Huge fires rage for months. Thirty-three people and more than a billion animals die from the fires that devastate an area about the size of Pennsylvania.

SOUTHERN AFRICA, WINTER 2020

After an extreme drought, the situation in southern African countries comes to a head. Animals die of thirst, and people are short of food and water.

9

ARCTIC HOTSPOT

WHERE IT'S WARMING FASTER THAN ANYWHERE ELSE.

Heat waves and expanding deserts, devastating hurricanes and floods—all around the world, people and places are being affected by climate change more than ever. But the place on our planet that is changing more drastically than anywhere else as a result of climate change is...

... THE ARCTIC.

What?

YOU MEAN THAT FARAWAY ICY AREA AROUND THE NORTH POLE IS BEING CALLED THE HOTSPOT OF HUMAN-CAUSED CLIMATE CHANGE?

In fact, the Arctic is warming at least twice as fast as the rest of the world, especially during the coldest months of the year. In the winter, when it can actually go down to -45°C (-49°F) in the Arctic, the WARMING is even more dramatic than in the summer!

An increase of the globally averaged temperature of 2°C (3.6°F) is the absolute maximum that our world can tolerate without the damage caused by climate change becoming much worse. That's why people everywhere are trying to prevent the temperature from rising by more than 1.5°C (2.7°F). But we are often way past that limit in the Arctic, such as in the Svalbard archipelago, located in the far north between mainland Norway and the North Pole.

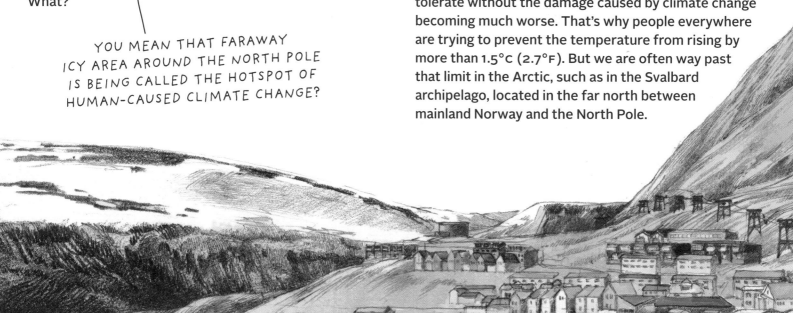

IN WINTER:
RAIN ON POLAR BEAR ISLAND

Svalbard is known for its icy glaciers, frozen tundra, and the bright northern lights dancing in the sky. And it's known for POLAR BEARS. There are so many of them that you can't leave the small settlements without protection. One of those villages, with its colorful wooden houses, is the village of Ny-Ålesund on the island of Spitsbergen, the northernmost settlement in Europe. Only researchers live here, and they see and measure how much climate change is transforming the Arctic every day.

This is particularly obvious in winter. Since the 1990s, the average temperature on the Svalbard island of Spitsbergen has risen by 6°C (10.8°F). When the researchers look out the windows of their colorful houses in winter today, it may be raining instead of snowing.

IN SUMMER:
THE ICE CONTINUES TO MELT

Satellite images show how the Arctic is changing. In the past, the sea ice stretched far over the Arctic Ocean even during the summer, lying like a wide white blanket among the continents of Asia, Europe, and North America. Today the ice is retreating farther and farther. Now in the summer, it takes up only half the area that it covered forty years ago.

So now you might ask:
WHAT DOES ALL THIS HAVE TO DO WITH US?

After all, the area around the North Pole is just a faraway, empty desert of ice. Or a sea with no ice. So what?

When climate change reshapes the Arctic so dramatically, the ENVIRONMENT of the people and animals that make their home there changes much more than some people realize. And these changes have an impact on the weather in Europe, Asia, and North America. So people around the entire world are affected. We all are.

11

THE WORLD'S WEATHER KITCHEN

The Arctic seems far, far away. But as the great naturalist and explorer Alexander von Humboldt said almost 250 years ago, in the natural world, everything is connected. So the changes that take place in the Arctic have more to do with the rest of us than many people think.

The Arctic is the "weather kitchen" of the Earth's northern hemisphere. What happens there affects the weather in Europe, North America, or Asia within days, weeks, or even months. The Arctic affects the day-to-day WEATHER. But it also influences the long-term CLIMATE in what we call the "moderate northern latitudes," where the winters are cold but not extremely icy, and the summers are warm without being extremely hot—exactly right for lots of different kinds of plants and animals. And pleasant living conditions for us humans, too.

Not everybody likes windy days. But we owe our balanced climate to the wind—particularly the westerly wind band that wraps around the northern hemisphere. High up in the atmosphere, fast-flowing winds of up to 500 kilometers (311 miles) per hour blow from the west around the Earth. This wind band is called the jet stream. Here on Earth you can often feel the lower reaches of the JET STREAM if you point your nose to the westerly wind.

"WHAT HAPPENS IN THE ARCTIC DOES NOT STAY IN THE ARCTIC." — MARKUS REX, POLARSTERN EXPEDITION LEADER

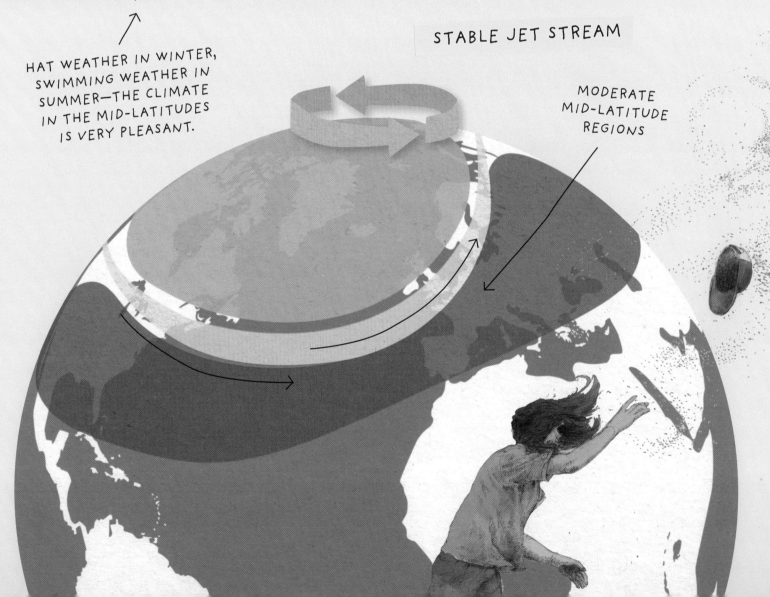

HAT WEATHER IN WINTER, SWIMMING WEATHER IN SUMMER—THE CLIMATE IN THE MID-LATITUDES IS VERY PLEASANT.

STABLE JET STREAM

MODERATE MID-LATITUDE REGIONS

The jet stream lies right between the Arctic and moderate latitudes. It is driven by the large temperature difference between the ice-cold air in the north and the milder air of the mid-latitudes. The jet stream acts like a barrier. It's like a fast-flowing river of wind that keeps the cold of the Arctic in the north separate from the warmer air of the temperate latitudes where we live.

But climate change is changing the jet stream. As temperatures rise in the north, especially in the Arctic, there is less temperature difference in the air on either side of the jet stream.

This causes the jet stream to move in waves over the northern hemisphere. And this MEANDERING of the wind band has grown stronger since the beginning of the industrial age, in the mid-eighteenth century.

As a result of these snaking wind movements, more hot air from the southern latitudes reaches us. Then it can get noticeably hot for over a longer period of time. Many parts of the world had such a heat wave in the summer of 2019, just before the *Polarstern* set out on her Arctic expedition. The summer of 2019 was the third hottest summer on record. It was so warm that nuclear power plants had to be switched off in Germany and France because their cooling systems could not be guaranteed. The city of Cambridge in the United Kingdom set a new heat record of 38.7°C (101.7°F). (Most schools in the U.K. close when the temperature goes higher than 26°C [79°F]!)

Climate change often results in weeklong HEAT WAVES like this. But it can also have surprising effects. When the jet stream meanders, ice-cold air from the Arctic can flow down to us in the south as well. Parts of the U.S. felt a COLD SNAP in the winter of 2019, before the *Polarstern* set off on its expedition. In January, Chicago was at -22°C (-7.6°F)! Due to the icy wind, the temperature actually felt like -46°C (-50.8°F). This is no longer just hat-and-mitten weather. Low temperatures like these are life-threatening.

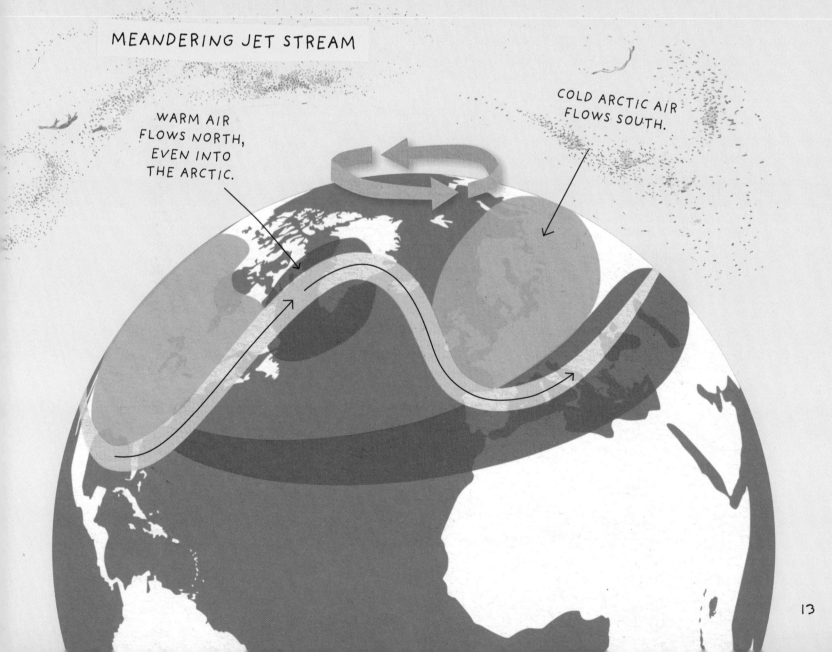

MEANDERING JET STREAM

WARM AIR FLOWS NORTH, EVEN INTO THE ARCTIC.

COLD ARCTIC AIR FLOWS SOUTH.

SECRETS OF THE POLAR NIGHT

For almost half the year the polar night plunges the North Pole into darkness. The moon and stars provide the only natural light during these long winter months. In the moonlight, the marine world looks like the bizarre, color-less landscape of another planet. Freezing cold and fierce storms break over the Arctic, making it one of the most hostile places on Earth. The *Polarstern* ventures into the middle of this unexplored and extremely cold darkness, because what goes on during the polar night is one of the biggest mysteries of the climate system. Only out here will the expedition find answers to the question: What is happening to the climate?

The Earth's CLIMATE SYSTEM is like a huge complicated puzzle. It has an infinite number of individual parts that are all interconnected. If pieces of the puzzle change or if they are changed, say, by us humans, the other pieces no longer fit together. And if some changes are big enough, they can seriously affect the whole climate-system puzzle.

Ever since science recognized that we humans have trig-gered climate change, scientists have been looking for all the parts that are now changing in the climate puzzle. Researchers around the world collect as much climate data as possible, which they then put together with a lot of brainpower and sophisticated computer programs. This is how they create CLIMATE MODELS.

MODELS OF THE CLIMATE PUZZLE

A climate model is a kind of forecast. It looks at the whole climate puzzle and predicts what the puzzle will look like in the future if one piece or another changes. The more we know about the pieces and the more precise the data that is fed into the climate model, the more accurate the PREDICTIONS will be.

HOW MUCH WILL THE EARTH WARM UP BY THE END OF THE TWENTY-FIRST CENTURY? WHAT ROLE WILL THE ARCTIC PLAY?

Climate models help us to answer such questions. They can be used to predict how climate change will change the Earth. And that is very important. We can only prepare ourselves for the consequences of climate change, such as extreme weather, if we know exactly what to expect. We can figure out the right steps to take to try to stop global warming because climate models can also show us what will happen if humanity just carries on as before.

SHOULD WE REALLY LET IT COME TO THIS?

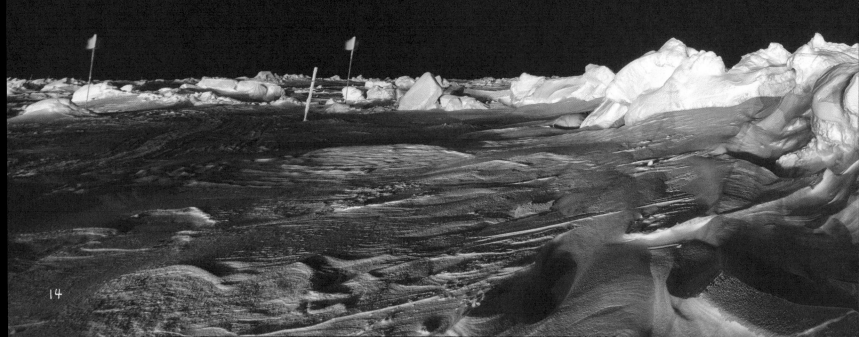

THE MISSING PIECE OF THE CLIMATE PUZZLE

Before the *Polarstern* expedition, there was a big piece missing from the climate puzzle. Scientists hadn't gathered enough data from the Arctic, particularly during the polar night. For science, the region around the North Pole had been the big blind spot. Nobody knew exactly how the climate system at the North Pole worked, or how it would change as a result of climate change.

The missing piece is due to the POLAR NIGHT. When the sun doesn't rise above the horizon during this time, the temperature can drop to a frosty -45°C (-49°F). The sea ice is so thick that not even a research icebreaker can get through it. Night and ice have locked science out of the Arctic winter so far.

So until now, climate models have had to do a lot of guesswork when they included the Arctic in their forecasts. However, the sea ice, the Arctic Ocean, the polar atmosphere, and even the Arctic ecosystem all affect the climate. But each climate model presents this relationship a little differently, using guesswork to fill in the gaps in data. This means some climate models predict that the Arctic will warm by 5°C (9°F) by the end of this century if we continue to emit greenhouse gases as usual. Others predict a full 15°C (27°F) of warming! It's as if the weather forecasters were to announce that tomorrow might be either 5°C (9°F) warmer than today, or 15°C (27°F) degrees warmer! Who would know what to wear?

This guesswork must come to an end. That's why the *Polarstern* set out for the Arctic to uncover the missing piece of the climate puzzle. This is the most important mission of the expedition: to solve the puzzles of the polar night and to collect the urgently needed data in the darkness so that scientists can use their models to reliably predict the climate.

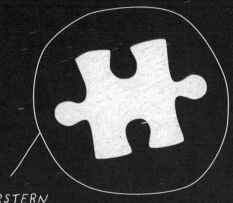

THE POLARSTERN
EXPEDITION HAS TO FIND
THE MISSING PIECE.

CAUGHT IN THE ICE

During the long polar night, massive pack ice prevents even the strongest icebreakers from reaching the North Pole. In the past it has forced many expedition ships to turn back—while others got trapped or even smashed by the mighty forces of the ice. Nevertheless, the *Polarstern* will go deep into the Central Arctic in the middle of the polar night.

THIS PLAN CAN ONLY SUCCEED IF HUMANS AND THE SHIP WORK WITH NATURE INSTEAD OF AGAINST IT.

When the sea ice has melted back and shrunk to its smallest area in September, the *Polarstern* looks for its way into the ice off the Siberian coast. Then the captain of the ship does something that everyone else tries to avoid. He switches the *Polarstern*'s engines to idle and lets his ship freeze in the Arctic sea ice.

FROM THIS POINT ON, NATURE WILL DETERMINE THE SHIP'S COURSE.

Surrounded by ice, the *Polarstern* will drift across the Arctic Ocean for many months. No helmsman will keep the ship on course. Instead, nature itself becomes the navigator. The ice will take the ship first toward the North Pole and then back south on the other side of the Arctic—at least, that's the plan. When it emerges, the *Polarstern* should arrive in the Fram Strait, the passage between Greenland and Svalbard, after a yearlong journey with the sea ice. By then she will have crossed the Arctic, with the expedition having observed over a full year what is going on in the Arctic climate system.

THE HULL OF THE POLARSTERN MUST BE STURDY ENOUGH TO STOP THE ICE FROM CRUSHING THE SHIP.

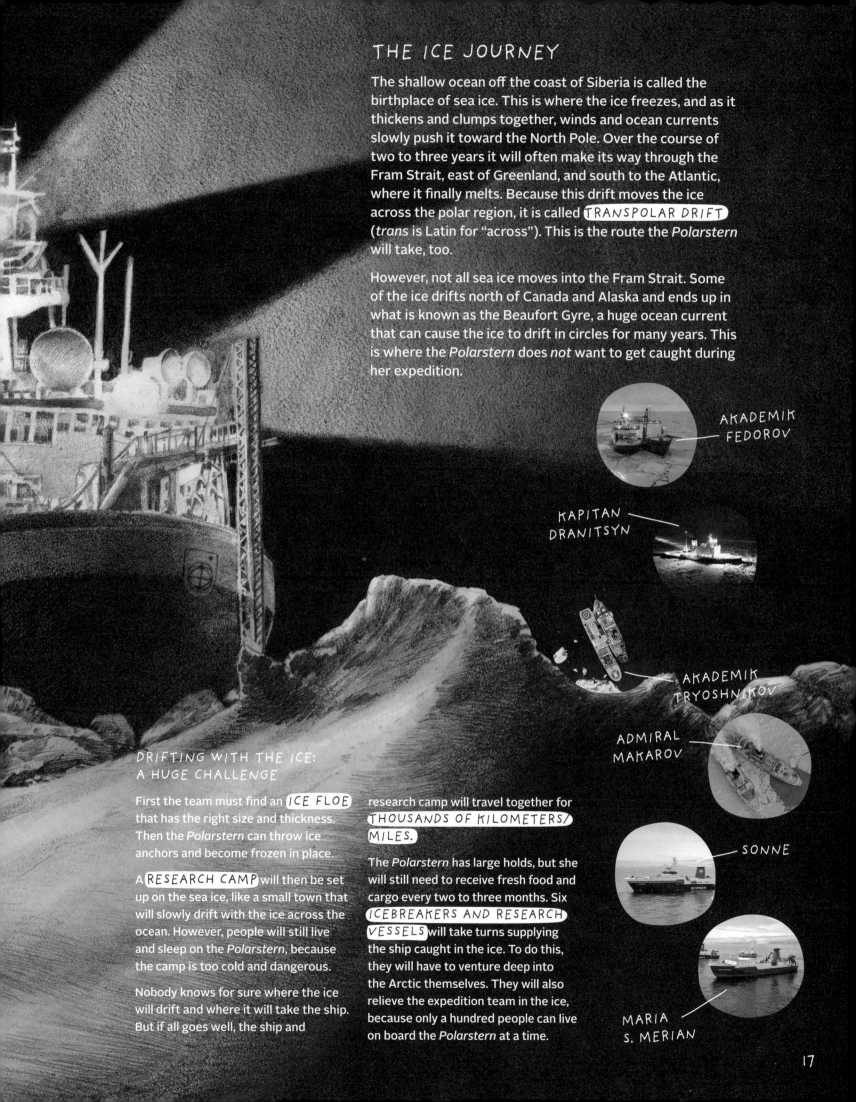

THE ICE JOURNEY

The shallow ocean off the coast of Siberia is called the birthplace of sea ice. This is where the ice freezes, and as it thickens and clumps together, winds and ocean currents slowly push it toward the North Pole. Over the course of two to three years it will often make its way through the Fram Strait, east of Greenland, and south to the Atlantic, where it finally melts. Because this drift moves the ice across the polar region, it is called TRANSPOLAR DRIFT (*trans* is Latin for "across"). This is the route the *Polarstern* will take, too.

However, not all sea ice moves into the Fram Strait. Some of the ice drifts north of Canada and Alaska and ends up in what is known as the Beaufort Gyre, a huge ocean current that can cause the ice to drift in circles for many years. This is where the *Polarstern* does *not* want to get caught during her expedition.

AKADEMIK FEDOROV

KAPITAN DRANITSYN

AKADEMIK TRYOSHNIKOV

ADMIRAL MAKAROV

SONNE

DRIFTING WITH THE ICE: A HUGE CHALLENGE

First the team must find an ICE FLOE that has the right size and thickness. Then the *Polarstern* can throw ice anchors and become frozen in place.

A RESEARCH CAMP will then be set up on the sea ice, like a small town that will slowly drift with the ice across the ocean. However, people will still live and sleep on the *Polarstern*, because the camp is too cold and dangerous.

Nobody knows for sure where the ice will drift and where it will take the ship. But if all goes well, the ship and research camp will travel together for THOUSANDS OF KILOMETERS/ MILES.

The *Polarstern* has large holds, but she will still need to receive fresh food and cargo every two to three months. Six ICEBREAKERS AND RESEARCH VESSELS will take turns supplying the ship caught in the ice. To do this, they will have to venture deep into the Arctic themselves. They will also relieve the expedition team in the ice, because only a hundred people can live on board the *Polarstern* at a time.

MARIA S. MERIAN

THE ICE DRIFT

NORTH STAR →

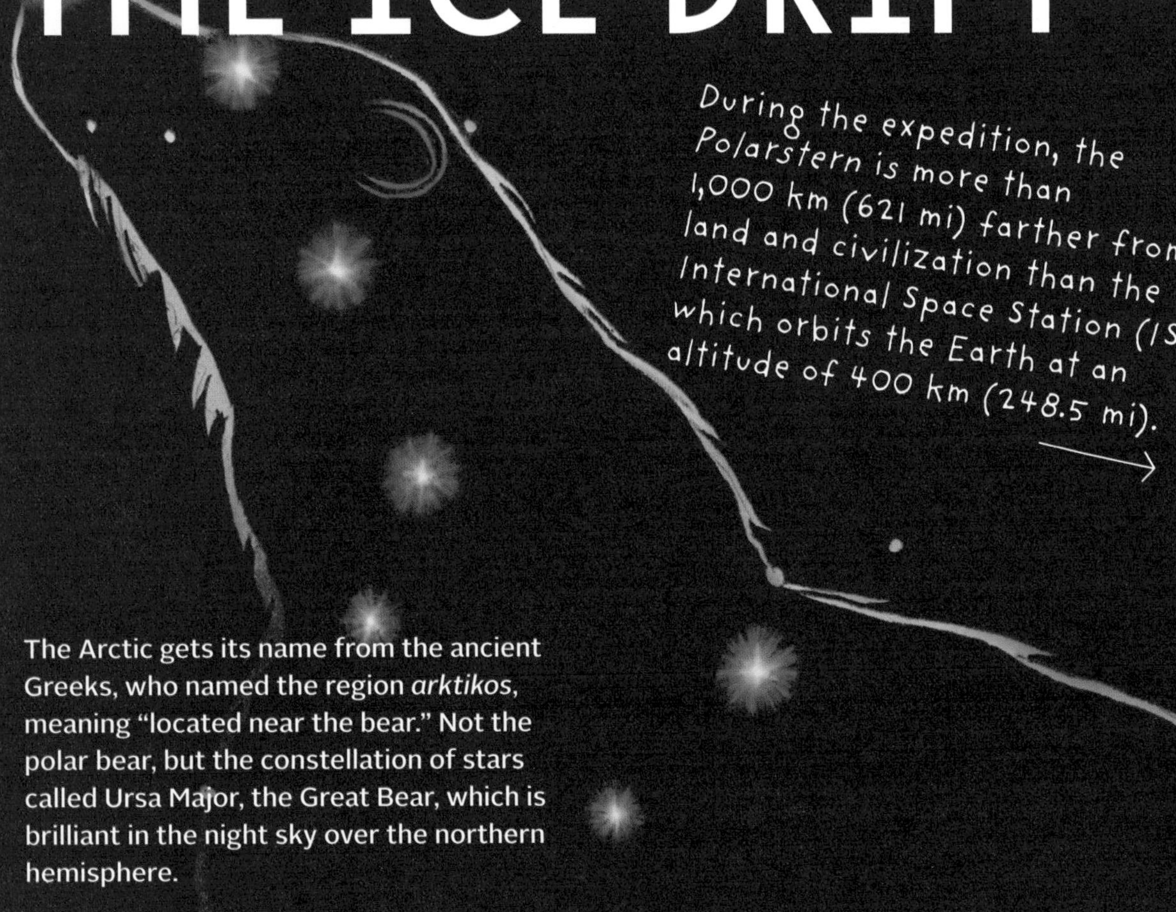

During the expedition, the Polarstern is more than 1,000 km (621 mi) farther from land and civilization than the International Space Station (ISS), which orbits the Earth at an altitude of 400 km (248.5 mi).

IN GERMAN, POLARSTERN MEANS NORTH STAR, REFERRING TO THE STAR THAT ALWAYS LIES DUE NORTH.

The Arctic gets its name from the ancient Greeks, who named the region *arktikos*, meaning "located near the bear." Not the polar bear, but the constellation of stars called Ursa Major, the Great Bear, which is brilliant in the night sky over the northern hemisphere.

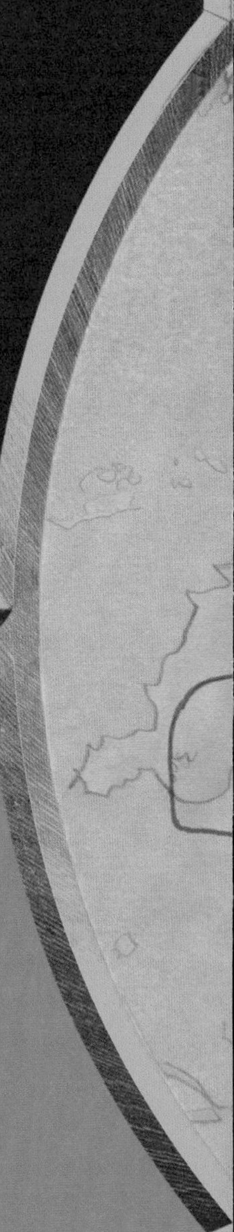

THE POLAR DAY LASTS FOR ONE DAY AT THE ARCTIC CIRCLE AND ALMOST HALF A YEAR AT THE NORTH POLE.

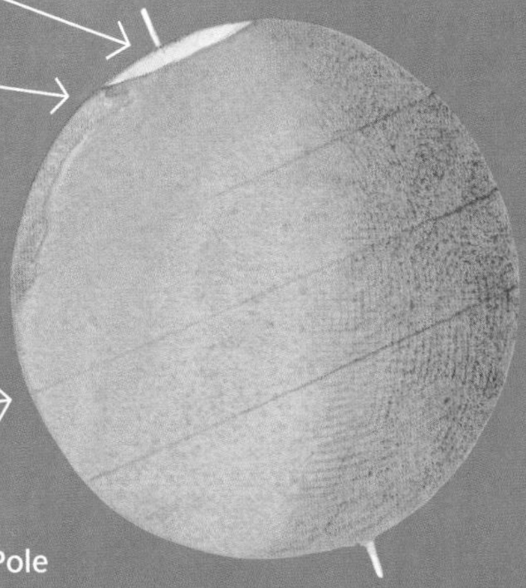

NORTH POLE

ARCTIC CIRCLE

EQUATOR

During the summer months, the *Polarstern* travels through the light of the polar day, when the "midnight sun" is in the sky for twenty-four hours a day. Polar day and polar night arise because the Earth's axis is tilted. Although the Earth rotates on its axis, the North Pole faces the sun for months during the summer; during the winter polar night, the North Pole faces away from the sun, and the sun remains below the horizon.

THE MIDNIGHT SUN NEVER SETS.

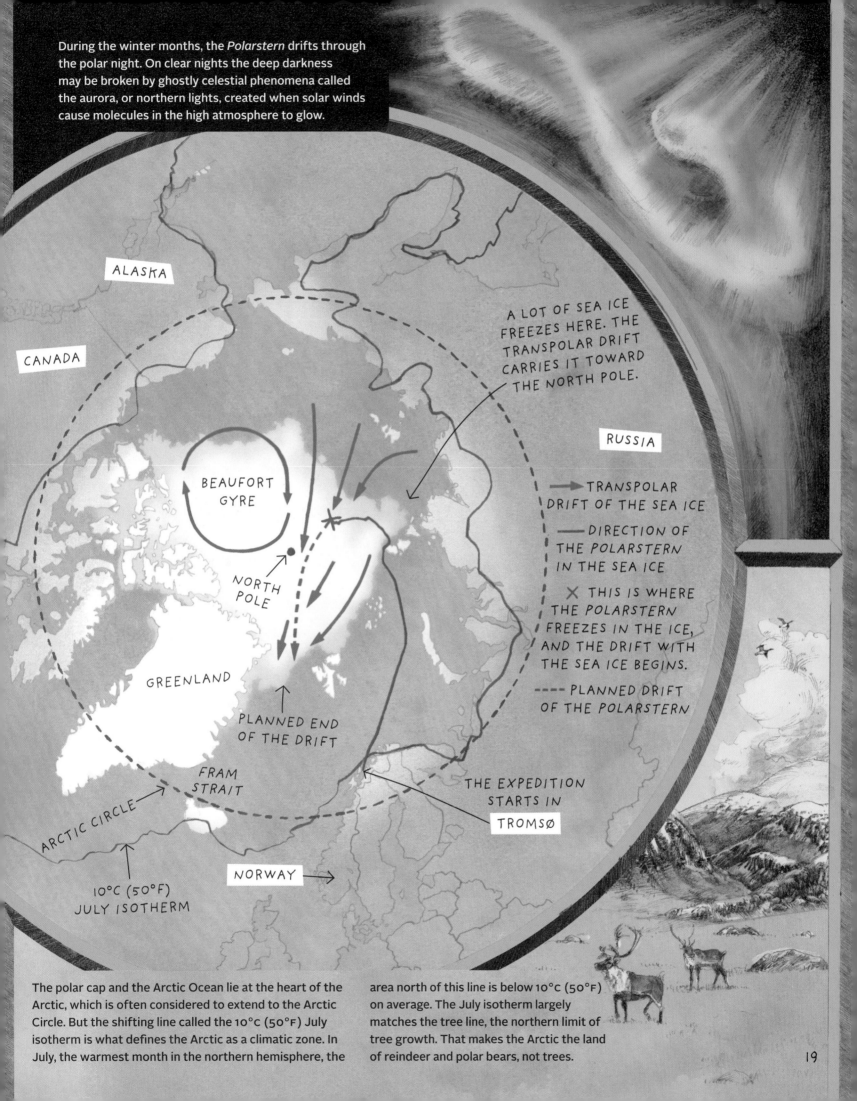

During the winter months, the *Polarstern* drifts through the polar night. On clear nights the deep darkness may be broken by ghostly celestial phenomena called the aurora, or northern lights, created when solar winds cause molecules in the high atmosphere to glow.

ALASKA

CANADA

A LOT OF SEA ICE FREEZES HERE. THE TRANSPOLAR DRIFT CARRIES IT TOWARD THE NORTH POLE.

RUSSIA

BEAUFORT GYRE

NORTH POLE

→ TRANSPOLAR DRIFT OF THE SEA ICE

— DIRECTION OF THE POLARSTERN IN THE SEA ICE

✕ THIS IS WHERE THE POLARSTERN FREEZES IN THE ICE, AND THE DRIFT WITH THE SEA ICE BEGINS.

--- PLANNED DRIFT OF THE POLARSTERN

GREENLAND

PLANNED END OF THE DRIFT

THE EXPEDITION STARTS IN TROMSØ

FRAM STRAIT

ARCTIC CIRCLE

NORWAY →

10°C (50°F) JULY ISOTHERM

The polar cap and the Arctic Ocean lie at the heart of the Arctic, which is often considered to extend to the Arctic Circle. But the shifting line called the 10°C (50°F) July isotherm is what defines the Arctic as a climatic zone. In July, the warmest month in the northern hemisphere, the area north of this line is below 10°C (50°F) on average. The July isotherm largely matches the tree line, the northern limit of tree growth. That makes the Arctic the land of reindeer and polar bears, not trees.

19

THE DISCOVERER OF ICE DRIFTING

SINKING OF THE USS JEANNETTE, JUNE 1881.

The idea of carrying a ship over the North Pole using the natural movement of the ice is not new. More than 125 years ago, the Norwegian scientist and explorer **Fridtjof Nansen** had the same idea.

Nansen wanted to be the first person to reach the North Pole. Before this, no one had gone that far into the Arctic ice. But Nansen was convinced that TRANSPOLAR DRIFT—the natural movement of the ice over the Arctic Ocean—existed, even if this was an unproven theory at that time. And so he planned the first drift expedition in history.

When Nansen said he wanted to freeze his ship in the PACK ICE, his contemporaries thought his plan was totally ridiculous. What an outlandish—and dangerous!—idea. However, Nansen had found good evidence that his plan might succeed.

In 1879 an American ship named the USS JEANNETTE set off from the Bering Strait for the North Pole. The ship didn't get far, at least not in one piece, because it was crushed by the pack ice. Some time later, a checkbook, a cap, and the provisions list from the ship were found in the ice. But they were discovered on the other side of the Arctic, at the southwestern tip of Greenland, thousands of nautical miles away.

That made Nansen think. How was this possible? The remnants must have migrated across the ocean with a current. At least, that was a theory that Nansen enthusiastically shared. Because thanks to this current, it suddenly seemed possible to travel to the North Pole, which at that time people knew less about than the surface of the moon. They could see the moon through telescopes, but no one had seen the North Pole. Strange legends grew up that seem like wild imaginings to us today. One even told of a kind of Garden of Eden that was fed by hot ocean currents!

WRECKAGE FROM THE USS JEANNETTE FOUND, JUNE 1884.

Nansen is considered to be the "discoverer" of ice drifting, and his journey over the Arctic Ocean is the historical inspiration for the *Polarstern* expedition.

L. Bacinski
CHRISTIANIA
CARL JOHANSGADE 20¾

PLANNED ROUTE OF THE FRAM, 1893.

Nansen was ambitious, and he was not discouraged by the skepticism of his contemporaries. What he needed, of course, was a special ship and a good crew. Otherwise his expedition would fail, too. The Arctic pack ice had already destroyed many ships and their crews. Together with the famous shipbuilder Colin Archer, Nansen designed a true miracle ship—the FRAM (from the Norwegian word for "forward").

The wooden hull of the *Fram* would be smooth and rounded so that the pressure of the pack ice would lift it up instead of crushing it. The hull would "slip like an eel out of the embraces of the ice," as Nansen himself described it. The idea was clever, but it didn't mean the *Fram* was beautiful. She was bulky and plump, and being a modern ship, was driven by a steam engine.

SO FAR SO GOOD. BUT WOULD NANSEN'S BOLD UNDERTAKING SUCCEED?

THE BOLD VOYAGE OF THE *FRAM*

In June 1893, Nansen, just thirty-two years old, set sail with a crew of twelve. **The *Fram* was soon frozen in the ice, but it did not break apart, and it actually began to drift.**

When Nansen realized that the ship was just drifting in a circle, he plunged into a deep depression, thinking his career as a discoverer and scientist was ruined. But in the end the ship changed direction, and the bold plan worked. The rounded hull of the *Fram* was lifted up by the pack ice and practically rode across the sea ice, carrying NANSEN'S EXPEDITION farther north than any ship had been before. It was a breakthrough success for the Norwegian scientist.

The *Fram* was a cleverly constructed ship. Its outer wall was fitted with thermal insulation made of tarred felt, cork, fir wood paneling, and airtight linoleum. Whether the temperature was 0°C (32°F) or -30°C (-22°F), Nansen boasted that they did not have to heat the ship on their journey through the Arctic. The *Fram* proved to be such a suitable expedition ship that the famous explorer Roald Amundsen later took her to the South Pole. The wonder ship had only one disadvantage. Because

of her stubby shape, the *Fram* swayed so much in the swell that even the toughest sailors regularly suffered from terrible seasickness.

Nansen's famous drift expedition yielded the discovery of a treasure trove of scientific—mostly oceanographic—data.

Before the *Fram* expedition, scientists thought the Arctic Ocean was shallow. To measure the depth, Nansen's crew lowered a plumb line. They were amazed when they had to tie together every rope and wire on board because the plumb bob didn't hit the bottom for a long time. It only touched bottom at almost 4,000 meters (4,374 yards)—a huge surprise for the explorers!

Nansen was a clever man and drew conclusions that could be described as the beginning of today's climate research. He thought that if the ocean was that deep, then there was a lot more water in the far north than expected. And that had to mean that the Arctic Ocean was also much more important to the Earth's climate than scientists had thought.

Nansen realized that we still had a long way to go before we understood the world's oceans—and especially the Arctic.

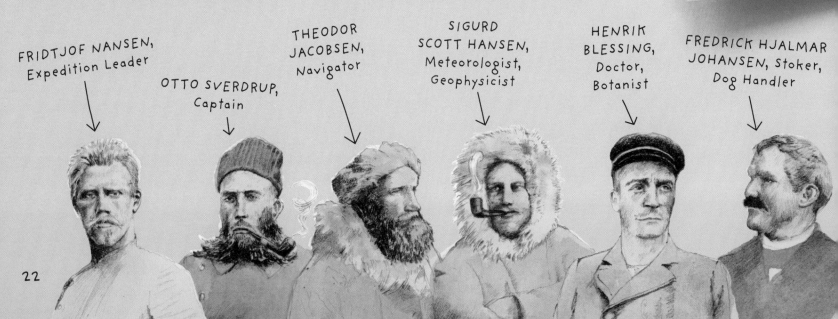

FRIDTJOF NANSEN, Expedition Leader

OTTO SVERDRUP, Captain

THEODOR JACOBSEN, Navigator

SIGURD SCOTT HANSEN, Meteorologist, Geophysicist

HENRIK BLESSING, Doctor, Botanist

FREDRICK HJALMAR JOHANSEN, Stoker, Dog Handler

A WINDMILL ON DECK SUPPLIED THE FRAM WITH ELECTRICITY.

IVAR MOGSTAD,
Mechanic

LARS PETTERSON,
Engineer

BERNT BENTSEN,
Roustabout

ADOLF JUELL,
Ship's Cook

ANTON AMUNDSEN,
Head Engineer

PEDER HENDRIKSEN,
Harpooneer

BERNHARD NORDAHL,
Electrician

NANSEN'S DARING TRIP TOWARD THE NORTH POLE

Nansen could have been quite satisfied with his successful drift through the Arctic Ocean by early 1895, but there was a catch. The plan to reach the North Pole did not seem to be working. The *Fram* had been out for eighteen months when Nansen learned they were drifting south again, away from the North Pole!

He immediately devised the next step in his ambitious plan. Accompanied by his crew member Hjalmar Johansen and twenty-eight dogs, and equipped with kayaks and three sledges, he left the *Fram*. Believe it or not, Nansen and Johansen had decided to make their way to the North Pole on foot.

For weeks the two men trudged north through the ice. Day after day they jumped from ice floe to ice floe with their equipment. They survived encounters with polar bears. They were almost sunk in their kayak when a walrus rammed its tusk right through the hull.

Nevertheless, at the beginning of April 1895 they had to give up with heavy hearts. They couldn't beat the ice. They had to go all the way back, but to where? After all, the *Fram* had long since drifted on.

After an arduous tour, they finally came to the Franz Josef Land archipelago. At least they had made it this far before the start of the polar night, when darkness would have meant certain death. Taking shelter in a hole in the ground, protected by driftwood and walrus hides, they survived the cold of winter. They ate polar bear and walrus meat. At first they fed the weak dogs to the others (which they had known they might have to do), but gradually the dogs all died.

SUGGEN
FLINT
STORRÆVEN
FREIA
SJØLIGET
BJELKI
BARRABAS
SULTAN
PAN
RUSSEN
ULENKA
KATTA
KVIK
BARO
BLOK
BARNET
HAREN
KAIFAS
GULEN
BARBARA
LILLERÆVEN
ISBJØRN
PERPETUUM
NARRIFAS
KVINDFOLKET
POTIFAR
LIVJÆGEREN
KLAPPERSLANGEN

Shortly before they planned to set off again, their kayaks broke loose with all their gear on board. Nansen knew this would be the end of them, so he jumped into the icy water, rescued the kayaks, and allegedly even killed a couple of auks for dinner while he was at it.

AT LEAST, THAT'S WHAT NANSEN WROTE IN HIS DIARY!

Despite the hardships, Nansen and Johansen survived fifteen long months together in the ice. Although they were lost in one of the most desolate places in the world, another expedition came by. At the sight of the long-lost, wild-looking explorer, the leader reportedly called out, "Are you Nansen? I am glad to see you!"

RESCUE
ON AN ISLAND

Franz Josef Land is the northernmost archipelago in the world. In Nansen's time this was a lonely, frozen group of islands populated mainly by polar bears. The hole where the two explorers took shelter still exists today, with the remains of driftwood, a bear bone, and a meager meal. But Franz Josef Land itself has changed. The greenhouse effect has pushed the sea ice, which used to block the way for ships in summer, much farther north.

AFTER A THREE-YEAR DRIFT EXPEDITION, THE FRAM AND HER TEAM ALSO ARRIVED HOME SAFE AND SOUND.

NOTES FROM THIN ICE

← FROM THE POLARSTERN

⚓

DATE: September 20, 2019, DAY 1

POSITION: 69° north, 18° east

TEMPERATURE: 5.6°C (42.1°F)

Cast off! In the port of the Norwegian city of Tromsø, our friends and families wave goodbye as we set off on the *Polarstern*. Our destination: the Central Arctic. The expedition veterans among us are just as excited as the newcomers. Will our drift experiment succeed, as we follow in the footsteps of Fridtjof Nansen from more than 125 years ago?

DATE: September 22, 2019, DAY 3

POSITION: 75° north, 44° east

TEMPERATURE: 1.2°C (34.2°F)

Last night the northern lights danced beautifully in the sky above us. And our journey is about to take us even farther north.

DATE: September 25, 2019, DAY 6

POSITION: 81° north, 107° east

TEMPERATURE: −1.3°C (29.7°F)

The cracking can be heard all over the ship. We have reached the end of the open water. The *Polarstern* is now carefully breaking its way through the sea ice.

DATE: September 27, 2019, DAY 8

POSITION: 82° north, 119° east

TEMPERATURE: −2.1°C (28.2°F)

Icebreaker rendezvous! Today we met with our Russian support ship *Akademik Fedorov*. With the help of satellite images, we are now looking for a suitable ice floe where we can freeze the *Polarstern* in the ice. How long will it take before we succeed?

DATE: September 29, 2019, DAY 10

POSITION: 84° north, 136° east

TEMPERATURE: −4.7°C (23.5°F)

We keep flying over the sea ice by helicopter. Our pilots are absolute professionals who land carefully on the ice floes. Then science teams venture out onto the ice and use ice drills to test the thickness of the floe. We haven't been successful yet. The ice is even thinner than some of us expected.

DATE: September 30, 2019, DAY 11

POSITION: 85° north, 137° east

TEMPERATURE: −7°C (19.4°F)

We are still looking for a suitable floe. So far each one has been too thin and fragile to carry our research camp. It's not surprising, since last summer was one of the warmest ever recorded in the Arctic.

DATE: October 1, 2019, DAY 12

POSITION: 85° north, 136° east

TEMPERATURE: −7.1°C (19.2°F)

We continue to explore floes, but still no success. Our team comes from all over the world, but no matter which language people speak, we are all talking about one thing: the dwindling sea ice.

DATE: October 4, 2019, DAY 15

POSITION: 85° north, 137° east

TEMPERATURE: −13.4°C (7.9°F)

The satellite image of one ice floe looked promising. And indeed: We have found our floe! In the coming months it will not only be the object of our research, but also our home. We had to carefully break into the floe with the ship. Now the ice anchors are thrown, and the *Polarstern* begins to freeze into the ice. Our drift has started!

DATE: October 6, 2019, DAY 17

POSITION: 85° north, 133° east

TEMPERATURE: −7.8°C (18°F)

During our first steps onto the floe, the sun blinked over the horizon before sinking again for a long time. Now begins our race against the coming of the polar night. We have to build the ice camp before it turns completely dark.

DATE: October 9, 2019, DAY 20

POSITION: 84° north, 135° east

TEMPERATURE: −14.3°C (6.3°F)

We use flags to mark safe routes on the ice. The wind makes our work difficult. It is getting darker and colder.

DATE: October 11, 2019, DAY 22

POSITION: 84° north, 135° east

TEMPERATURE: −12.3°C (9.9°F)

A female polar bear and her cub inspected the camp today. We had to evacuate the ice—and yet we were fascinated by their visit!

DATE: October 17, 2019, DAY 28

POSITION: 84° north, 132° east

TEMPERATURE: −14.8°C (5.4°F)

When we were at work just now, we heard a strange noise—and a crack opened up right through our ice floe. We'll have to keep a close eye on it.

DATE: October 24, 2019, DAY 35

POSITION: 85° north, 128° east

TEMPERATURE: −15.3°C (4.5°F)

Done! We set up camp just in time for the final nightfall. But our floe is restless, it cracks and creaks. Now as we begin our research we must always be on watch. The ice is constantly moving.

DATE: October 27, 2019, DAY 38

POSITION: 85° north, 126° east

TEMPERATURE: −22.6°C (−8.7°F)

Heading north! After we drifted in circles at first, the sea ice is now carrying us toward the North Pole!

27

THE ICEBREAKER
POLARSTERN

The *Polarstern* was put into service in 1982, which makes her an old hand. However, this is still one of the best research icebreakers in the world—the flagship of the Alfred Wegener Institute in Bremerhaven, and of all of Germany's polar research.

During the expedition, the ship will be a safe home for one hundred people in the middle of the Arctic ice. They will live, sleep, and eat here. But the *Polarstern* is also equipped with state-of-the-art instruments and various laboratories, and it will serve as a workplace for the scientists to conduct their research. Only icebreakers can break through pack ice and travel through such regions.

118 METERS (387 FEET) LONG

1 PROW
The *Polarstern* can break through sea ice 1.5 meters (4.9 feet) thick. In thicker ice, it rams through. The bow is reinforced with steel plates. Due to its thick steel shell, the *Polarstern* is very heavy, with a draft of 11 meters (36 feet). "Draft" is the minimum depth of water needed to keep a boat from hitting bottom.

2 FOOD STORES
Provides food for the one hundred people on board.

3 GALLEY
In the ship's kitchen, the cook team prepares delicious meals. Even the rolls at breakfast are freshly baked.

4 BLUE SALON
This is where important meetings take place. It also houses a library containing historical works on polar research.

5 MESS
This is the dining room and common room. Traditionally, sailors calls the dining room "the mess." Good food is very important on a strenuous sea expedition.

6 SICK BAY
The ship's doctor and nurse take care of anyone who is injured or sick. There is even a fully equipped operating room, because the expedition is too far from the mainland to fly people to the nearest hospital in case of an emergency.

7 OBSERVATION DECK
On the roof of the bridge, special instruments send and receive important navigational and scientific data to and from satellites.

8 CROW'S NEST
At the highest observation point on the *Polarstern*, people and technology can keep an eye on their surroundings and observe things like whales and the sea ice.

9 LABORATORIES
Researchers analyze data on board using various instruments.

10 ICE LAB CONTAINER
This is where the scientists' ice samples are stored at -20°C (-4°F). During the Arctic winter it can be warmer in here than it is outside.

11 WORKING DECK
Scientific equipment is launched here. To prevent slippery ice from forming, underfloor heating warms the planks.

12 WINCHES
They can be used to lower devices thousands of meters/ yards into the water.

13 LARGE CRANE
The crane can lift up to 25 tons onto the ice—from devices to containers and even snowplows.

14 ENGINE ROOM
The four main engines provide an impressive 20,000 horsepower. For comparison, a modern car has around 190 horsepower on average. A person pedaling a bicycle produces about 0.1 horsepower when riding comfortably.

15 CARGO HOLD
The hull can hold enormous amounts of cargo, and there is a sophisticated loading procedure to avoid confusion.

16 BRIDGE
The bridge is the command center, where the captain and his crew steer the ship and keep a constant eye on the sea and the ice.

17 LARGE SEARCHLIGHT
In the polar night the searchlights are one of the few but powerful sources of light.

18 WEATHER STATION
This is where the all-important weather forecasts are made. This is how the *Polarstern* crew knows whether they can work safely on the ice or whether a storm is approaching.

19 HELIPAD
There is space for two helicopters on the *Polarstern*.

25 METERS (82 FEET) WIDE

TEAM POLARSTERN

Polar expeditions are still a great adventure today. A healthy mix of courage, caution, and experience is important when you are exploring the extreme world of the Arctic. The *Polarstern* team is a motley crew. Its members represent all ages and come from all over the world and from a wide variety of professions.

HELICOPTER PILOT

DOCTOR
The on-board doctor is prepared for any emergency, whether it's a broken leg or a ruptured appendix.

METEOROLOGIST
Together with his colleagues, he has the important job of forecasting the weather.

GRADUATE STUDENT
One of the youngest people on board, building a career as a scientist and researcher.

LEADER, TEAM OCEAN

PHOTOGRAPHER
She records the expedition for future generations.

LEADER, TEAM ATMOSPHERE
Keeps track of the team's research.

BEAR GUARD

LEADER TEAM BIOCHEMISTR

CINEMATOGRAPHER

TWENTY COUNTRIES ARE REPRESENTED IN THE EXPEDITION, WHICH MAKES SENSE, SINCE CLIMATE CHANGE DOES NOT STOP AT NATIONAL BORDERS.

LEADER, TEAM SEA ICE
Coordinates ice research.

BEAR GUARD

HELICOPTER TECHNICIAN

CHIEF PILOT
To be a helicopter pilot in the Arctic, you have to be a real flying ace.

LOGISTICS MANAGER
Takes care of the cargo on board the ship and in the entire ice camp.

MOS
International Arctic Drift Expeditio

MACHINE CREW
Engineers and mechanics take care of the Polarstern's powerful diesel engines. The crew can tell by sound and touch how the motors are running.

SECOND OFFICER
Also the security expert, who keeps an eye out for danger.

NAVAL COMMUNICATOR
The communications officer, who looks after connections to the outside world, mostly via satellite.

CAPTAIN
The person responsible for the ship and crew, usually found on the bridge.

BAKER
Everyone loves this crew member, who makes all those rolls and cakes.

EXPEDITION LEADER
Being the head of the largest Arctic expedition ever means being in charge of many important decisions, whether about research or the setup of the ice camp.

FIRST OFFICER
Along with three navigators, who take turns doing watch duty on the bridge. These are the people who actually pilot the ship. The captain takes over only in difficult situations.

NURSE
The doctor's right hand, who will also handle smaller medical issues.

COOK
According to the sailors, the kitchen crew is the most important team on the ship!

DECKHANDS
Crew members who operate large equipment such as cranes and winches.

HEAD CHEF

LEADER TEAM ECOSYSTEM

EXPEDITION BANNER
Big expeditions have their own banner. The name of this expedition is MOSAiC. It fits with the mosaic of ice floes where the research camp is located.

STEWARD

LAUNDRY STAFF

BOATSWAIN
Looks after the Polarstern's technical equipment.

SYSMAN
The systems administrator, who oversees the ship's IT.

HEAD STEWARD
The leader of those who take care of the rest of the crew. The head steward also sells chocolate in the ship's kiosk!

BEAR GUARDS
There's always a guard on the ice to make sure the polar bears don't get too close.

31

YESTERDAY FUR COATS,

Good preparation is everything. After all, there's no hardware store or clothing shop at the North Pole for if you accidentally leave your ice drill or long underwear at home.

Nansen and his crew didn't have modern high-tech clothing. But they had carefully studied how the Indigenous people of the Arctic dressed. The "onion principle" protects against the cold. Cushions of air form between individual layers of clothing, which insulate against the cold.

Nansen was so warmly dressed that in 1894 he wrote in his diary:

"I am sweating like a horse!"

WOLFSKIN HOOD

SHIRT

SEALSKIN COAT

KNEE PANTS

STOCKINGS

SNOW SOCKS

FRIEZE GAITERS

FINNISH BOOTS

Nansen used sled dogs to travel across the ice. The *Polarstern* team, on the other hand, uses speedy snowmobiles. For longer distances, they rely on the helicopter. To save fuel, some people take the challenge of skiing over the ice floe.

TODAY HIGH-TECH ALL THE WAY

POLARSTERN RESEARCHER IN 2020

SAFETY GOGGLES

FACE MASK

HIGHLY VISIBLE RED OVERALLS WITH BUOYANCY FUNCTION, IN CASE YOU BREAK THROUGH THE ICE AND FALL IN THE WATER

SIGNAL WHISTLE TO CALL FOR HELP

THERMAL GLOVES

SNOW BOOTS WITH INNER LINING

FAKE FUR HAT

WARM UNDER-CLOTHING

THIN INNER GLOVES

LONG UNDERWEAR

WOOL SOCKS

THINGS YOU SHOULD ALWAYS TAKE WITH YOU ON THE ICE

ROPE: for rescue operations

KNIFE: always useful in the wilderness

HEADLAMP: handy for working in the dark polar night, to keep your hands free

SIGNAL PISTOL/RIFLE: to scare off polar bears

RADIO: to stay in contact with the *Polarstern*

PENCIL AND NOTE-PAD: because ballpoints don't work in the cold

THERMOS: so you can take a sip to warm up from time to time

CHOCOLATE: for a quick snack during strenuous work on the ice

LIFE ON BOARD
AN ICEBREAKER

OCTOBER 9, 2019

Polar research can be a backbreaking job. Dealing with brittle ice, storms, cold, polar bears, and trudging through deep snow is physically strenuous and means being constantly on guard. But the *Polarstern* also offers many opportunities to relax and have fun.

Hungry people get cold faster. A well-filled stomach is particularly important when you're working in the Arctic. Meals are served four times a day.

LOST MY KEY SOMEWHERE AROUND HERE

Menu

BREAKFAST
Freshly Baked Rolls With a Variety of Toppings, Granola

LUNCH
Meatballs or Vegetarian Meatballs With Roasted Potatoes and Vegetables

AFTERNOON SNACK
Coffee, Tea, and Cake

FRESHLY BAKED, OF COURSE

IF THERE ARE STILL SUPPLIES OF FRESH FOOD ON BOARD

DINNER
Freshly Baked Rolls With Cold Cuts and Vegetables

WEIGH-IN SUNDAYS

THE FOOD ON THE POLARSTERN IS SO GOOD THAT IT'S EASY TO PUT ON A LITTLE "EXPEDITION BLUBBER" WHILE LIVING ON BOARD. MEMBERS OF THE WEIGH-IN CLUB ESTIMATE THEIR WEIGHT BEFORE GETTING ON THE SCALE. IF YOU'RE WRONG, THE FINE IS 50 CENTS. WHEN WE GET HOME, WE'LL DONATE THE MONEY TO A GOOD CAUSE.

LONG-DISTANCE COUNTRY CODES

RUSSIA: +7
GERMANY: +49
SWEDEN: +46
NORWAY: +47
SWITZERLAND

USA: +1
JAPAN: +81
AUSTRIA: +43
BELGIUM: +32
DENMARK: +4
FINLAND: +35
FRANCE: +33
RLANDS: +31
D: +48
+34
D KINGDOM: +44
A: +1
KOREA: +82

CALLING FROM THE ARCTIC
Astronauts on the International Space Station (ISS) can talk to their families on Earth via videophone. However, due to the lack of satellites, the connection to the central Arctic is much worse than it is to the space station. After all, the *Polarstern* is farther away from civilization than the ISS is. We can only call our families at home on creaky satellite phones.

If you're thinking about helping the climate, choose a <u>meat-free dish</u>, because plant-based products are better for the planet.

FOUND KEY

9 JANUARY
THURSDAY
SAILOR'S SUNDAY

When you're at sea, Thursday is considered "Sailors' Sunday." On the *Polarstern* this means the food is especially yummy. In the morning you can have your eggs any way you like, whether fried or in an omelet. And today there will be ice cream for dessert!

LEAVE NO CRUMBS BEHIND! EATING ON THE ICE IS STRICTLY FORBIDDEN. LEFTOVER FOOD COULD ATTRACT POLAR BEARS!

POLAR PROVISIONS
To survive in the Arctic, we store huge amounts of food on board. Unfortunately, fresh fruit and vegetables are only available for a short time. However, in Europe, fresh eggs remain edible for months, especially if we turn them over every week.

TAKE A BREAK
The expedition crew works around the clock. But if you are looking for a change of pace, you have many options:

THE SAUNA IS A REAL TREAT AFTER A DAY OUT ON THE ICE.

DID EVERYONE SEE THAT AMAZING STARRY SKY YESTERDAY?

EGGS ALREADY TURNED, NOV. 11, —THE CAPTAIN

BUNK AND CABIN
Two crew members share a room, also called a cabin. Each cabin has its own bathroom with a shower. If you have to go to the toilet on the ice, you must use a special bag or return to the ship.

THANK GOODNESS THE WATER IS WARM!

JANUARY 12 PLEASE SIGN UP!

Browsing in the library: FOLKE M., SEBASTIAN G.

Waterbasketball in the pool: BJELA K., ESTHER H.

Sweating in the sauna: YING-CHIH, BORIS C.

Soccer on the ice in front of the *Polarstern*:

Presentation in the lecture hall: EGOR S., STEFFI A.

Stargazing:

Haircut: LISA G

PEEING OUT ON THE ICE IS STRICTLY FORBIDDEN!

ONLY IF YOU TRUST THE BOATSWAIN'S HAIRDRESSING SKILLS!

GOALIE WANTED!

35

WORKDAY ON THE ICE

An expedition day is long. There is also work on the weekends, and there is always something to do, especially for the crew that keeps the *Polarstern* going. And it can be dangerous out there on the sea ice. That's why it's important to follow the rules to the letter.

CAREFUL, IT'S SLIPPERY!

You can get onto the ship either via the gangway or, if the floe is very unstable, in a basket that the crane lifts onto the ice. This basket is called the "Mummy chair." But pay attention. Both the deck and the gangway can be slippery!

THE MOST IMPORTANT RULES OF THE EXPEDITION

- Safety comes first, always and everywhere!
- Stay calm.
- Have a Plan B, and preferably also a Plan C and a Plan D. In the Arctic, things can always turn out differently than you expect.
- Never go out on the ice alone.
- Always watch out for others.
- Eat, hydrate, and sleep well to stay fit.
- Before setting out, make sure your equipment is in good working order.

NEVER GO OUT ON THE ICE WITHOUT A BEAR GUARD!

When the ship's horn sounds, that means a polar bear alarm. Everyone must return to the ship immediately!

WARNING: IT'S COLD OUT THERE!

Polar bears may be impressive, but the most dangerous thing about the Arctic is the cold. Frostbite is one of the biggest risks during a polar expedition. The face and fingers are particularly vulnerable. At first, frostbite feels like pins and needles. The skin turns white and is cold and numb to the touch. In worse cases, it turns blue or even black, and the tissue dies. So the crew only ever goes out on deck or on the ice in full polar gear. Above all, protect your fingers and face well against the cold!

WATCH OUT FOR HYPOTHERMIA!

A low body temperature, known as "hypothermia," is life-threatening. It occurs when the core temperature of the body sinks below 35°C (95°F). After the initial shivering and feeling cold, those affected often become tired and listless. They no longer understand that they are freezing to death, which makes hypothermia even more dangerous. That's why nobody is allowed to go out on the ice alone.

COLDER THAN COLD—THINK ABOUT WINDCHILL!

In the Arctic it can get as cold as -45°C (-49°F). But if the wind hits the body and blows away the layer of warm air above the surface of the skin, it can feel much colder… -60°C (-76°F) or even colder if the wind is strong. This effect is called "wind-chill." Such extreme temperatures are not only felt as cold, but also as severe pain. So clothing should be as windproof as possible.

TAKE THE SURVIVAL KIT!

Every team that ventures far out onto the ice or even goes outside the research camp must carry a survival box. This might include a first aid kit, signal device, parachute signal rocket, sleeping bag, self-warming rescue blanket, dry suit, woolen hat, boots, socks, stove, emergency provisions, smoke signal, snow saw, cookware, floating flashlight, and stormproof matches. It also contains a signal mirror to attract the attention of aircraft.

KNOW WHERE YOU ARE!

With ice and ocean stretching out on all sides, it's easy to get lost in the Arctic, especially if the weather and visibility are poor. Night and fog can be truly impenetrable. So it is particularly important to observe the weather at all times and pay close attention to the weather report from the on-board meteorologists. The weather in the Arctic can change very quickly and anyone who strays too far from the ship or the given route can end up in a life-threatening situation. So our researchers invented IceNavi, a computerized navigational device that can also show the way back to the ship.

DAILY SCHEDULE

07:00	daily meeting with captain, scientific expedition leaders, officers, and doctor
07:30	breakfast in the mess
08:00	polar bear watch begins on the bridge
08:15	weather report meeting for work on the ice and helicopter flight operations
08:30	brief discussion: does the team have the green light for fieldwork?
08:35	gangway down: work begins out on the ice
11:30	lunch in the mess
13:00	return to work on the ice
15:30	coffee break on board to warm up and get some refreshments
17:30	latest return to the ship; the entire team must come back on board at this time
17:30	dinner in the mess
18:30	daily meeting with all researchers and the captain to plan further work
from 19:00	many other meetings take place

SIGNAL MIRROR WITH SIGHT LINE

TEAM CHANGE AT THE NORTH POLE

A year in the ice is a tremendously long time. The one hundred hardworking and hungry people on board also ensure that the *Polarstern*'s huge cargo holds and fuel tanks empty quickly.

THE POLARSTERN WAITS FOR ALMOST ONE HUNDRED NEW CREW MEMBERS AND RESEARCHERS AS WELL AS MORE THAN 40 TONS OF CARGO.

THE ICE IS NOW STABLE ENOUGH TO HOLD THE 16-TON SNOWCAT.

FOR THE PAST MONTH THE SUPPLY ICEBREAKER HAS FOUGHT ITS WAY FROM NORWAY TO THE *POLARSTERN* THROUGH EXCEPTIONALLY SOLID ICE (KNOWN AS "FAST SEA ICE").

Although the ship is carried along by the DRIFTING ICE, with the freezing temperatures outside, even the well-insulated *Polarstern* has to burn fuel to heat the ship. Other ships bring fuel and other supplies to the frozen icebreaker every two to three months. At the same time, the team will be replaced by a new crew. Such a meeting between ships in the middle of the sea ice requires sophisticated planning. And at one point it almost looks as though the ice will dash the plan altogether.

AT WHAT FEELS LIKE -58°C (-72°F), THE NEWCOMERS ARE HAPPY TO HEAD FOR THE WARMTH OF THE POLARSTERN.

THE CAPTAINS OF THE ICEBREAKERS GREET EACH OTHER.

FIGHTING THE ICE

In the middle of the polar night, the Russian supply ice-breaker KAPITAN DRANITSYN struggles to make its way forward. The sea ice is so solid that the ship can barely move. And the crew knows that even an icebreaker can fail on the pack ice. If the power of the huge machinery is not enough to drive the ship through the ice, the ship will try to RAM it. First it reverses, then picks up speed again and breaks into the ice with momentum. Many such attempts may be needed to advance through solid pack ice. To save energy, icebreakers tend to follow the cracks and channels that open up in the floe. And while the *Kapitan Dranitsyn* is slowly making its way forward, the ice drift has pushed the *Polarstern* to a new location, and the *Dranitsyn* has to set a new course.

ARRIVING AT THE ICE FLOE

The crew on the *Polarstern* is waiting nervously. Will the SUPPLY SHIP make it through the ice? Eventually, a bright light appears on the horizon. The *Kapitan Dranitsyn* has made it, thanks to the seafaring skills of the Russian captain and his crew. The supply ship slowly approaches the floe that holds the frozen *Polarstern*. Extra care must be taken not to damage the ice camp here. In the end, the Russian ship moors almost a kilometer (about half a mile) away. Now comes the next challenge. Will the crew, provisions, and equipment make it over the ice safely? The icy wind has made the temperature a freezing cold -58°C (-72°F).

Wrapped in many layers of polar clothing, the researchers shoulder their backpacks and set off on foot. POLAR BEAR GUARDS keep an eye out for the large predators, but in the past few months only a single bear has been spotted in the winter darkness. Snowmobiles and two snowcats are also used. They pull the heaviest cargo over the ice on sledges—a tricky procedure.

Everyone is happy when the exchange is complete a few days later. But what can the new team members expect on the ice? How does the equipment in the ice camp work? What's the best way to protect yourself from polar bears? The new team can receive valuable detailed instructions on how best to do their jobs. When the "old" crew finally has to say goodbye, many are sad to leave their home on the *Polarstern*. But the new team can be trusted to take the reins over the coming months—alone out there in the vastness of the Arctic.

CLIMATE RESEARCH ⊙N THE ICE

THE POLARSTERN MAKES HISTORY

Firmly surrounded by ice, the *Polarstern* drifts over the Arctic Ocean. Over the long winter months it travels through the freezing cold and pitch-black polar night. On February 24, 2020, it goes down in the history of polar research by setting a new record, reaching 88°36′ N, only 156 kilometers (97 miles) from the North Pole!

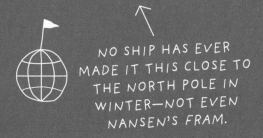

NO SHIP HAS EVER MADE IT THIS CLOSE TO THE NORTH POLE IN WINTER—NOT EVEN NANSEN'S FRAM.

RESEARCH IN THE DARK

During this time, the headlights of the *Polarstern* and the flashlights and headlamps of the expedition team are the only sources of light in the icy landscape. Beyond the lamps looms the absolute blackness of the POLAR NIGHT. Only when the moon shows up does the bizarre landscape of ice—which changes by the day—reveal itself. Under the black sky, the silvery-gray surroundings often look like the surface of the moon.

The researchers go to work every day. Neither the cold nor the often-violent wind, which turns snowflakes into small, stinging projectiles, keeps them from their work on the sea ice. With snowmobiles, wooden Nansen sleds, and skis, they make their way over the ice to the individual stations and measuring devices of the research camp. They may fly out in a helicopter to repair a measuring buoy that's drifting far away and has been disturbed by the sea ice. It's only when polar bears approach the camp or storms roar across the sea ice that they stay inside—to measure, document, and analyze samples in the ship's laboratories. The sea ice doesn't always make their work easy. Again and again the ice floe breaks apart under the force of the wind and ocean currents. Sometimes whole parts of the camp drift away with all the tents and equipment. When the researchers climb out of their bunks in the morning, the camp may look completely different than it did the night before.

But ice cracks and storms, drifting, and all the other interactions of sea ice, atmosphere, and ocean are exactly the events they have been waiting for. These are the things they can now explore in depth, for the first time in the history of polar exploration.

DRIFTING UNDER THE MIDNIGHT SUN

Finally, at the end of February, the first gentle streak of light appears on the horizon. The light gradually grows stronger and rosier, and finally the sun returns to the Arctic ice. From now on, the blazing MIDNIGHT SUN will be in the sky and will not set for half a year.

During the second half of the expedition, the researchers on the *Polarstern* work in the light. Their surroundings shine icy white and then, as the melting season begins, in more and more shades of blue and green. Under the light of the sun, color comes into the supposedly eternal white of the Arctic. That's when life explodes in this strange world.

The researchers study ice, snow, and the surface of the water. However, their measurements will also reach 4,297 meters (4,699 yards) below the ocean surface, and a full 36,278 meters (39,674 yards) into the atmosphere.

THE "GOOD" GREENHOUSE EFFECT

Climate research often revolves around the question of how climate change is altering the Earth due to the greenhouse effect, which is widely recognized as a problem. And for a good reason. But did you know that without the greenhouse effect there would be no life on our planet at all?

WHAT DOES A CLIMATE FORECASTER REALLY DO?

A weather forecaster watches the sky and predicts the weather for the next few days. "Weather" refers to the state of the atmosphere in a certain place at a certain time. The weather can change rapidly. It can be sunny today and rainy tomorrow. So weather is a short-term affair. The weather forecaster's colleague, the *climate* forecaster (who is unfortunately much less well known), on the other hand, has a very tedious task, because climate describes the average state of the atmosphere in a certain region over a longer period of time: from thirty years to centuries. So the climate forecaster must consider a much longer time span and knows that, for example, three cool years in a row does not mean the climate has become colder. It's too short a time period to draw this kind of conclusion.

It wasn't that long ago that scientists first started thinking about the "good" greenhouse effect. In 1824 a physicist named Joseph Fourier wondered about the Earth's temperature. He came to the conclusion that given the amount of solar radiation hitting the planet, the Earth should actually be much colder. But then, as now, the average temperature was around 15°C (59°F).

Fourier thought this was strange—until the answer to the riddle occurred to him. It had to have something to do with the Earth's gas envelope—the atmosphere. Fourier had discovered the so-called NATURAL GREENHOUSE EFFECT. We can blame this for the fact that our planet has such a life-friendly climate. And, as the name suggests, the Earth's atmosphere actually works in a similar way to a greenhouse.

NOT TOO HOT AND NOT TOO COLD—JUST RIGHT FOR DIVERSE LIFE.

HOW THE NATURAL GREENHOUSE EFFECT WORKS

1. The sun is the engine of the Earth's climate system. Its warmth sets everything in motion.

2. SOLAR RADIATION hits the Earth. The Earth's surface absorbs about half of the radiation, heats up, and in turn emits thermal radiation.

3. Without the Earth's gas envelope, this THERMAL RADIATION would disappear into space. Then it would actually be cold on Earth—with an average temperature of -18°C (0°F). In other words, our planet would be one big frozen lump.

4. But the Earth's gas envelope, the atmosphere, prevents this. The ATMOSPHERE contains so-called GREENHOUSE GASES such as water vapor (H_2O), carbon dioxide (CO_2), ozone (O_3), nitrous oxide (N_2O), and methane (CH_4). The thermal radiation hits these gases on its way back out into space. The gases absorb the rays and send a good portion of them back to Earth. This is how the lower layers of air and the ground warm up.

The natural greenhouse effect leads to a buildup of heat in the atmosphere, much like in a greenhouse with a glass roof. Thanks to this, our average global temperature is a pleasant 15°C (59°F)— a whopping 33°C (59.4°F) higher than it would be without the gas envelope.

WINDS carry warm air from the equator up to the poles, while the OCEAN CURRENTS move warm water.

As a result of solar radiation, water evaporates from the oceans, rivers, and lakes. Water vapor is created and it forms CLOUDS that produce rain or snow.

The ice-covered POLAR REGIONS are the refrigerators of the Earth. Unlike the Earth's surface on the rest of the world, they do not absorb the sun's rays, but reflect them and thus cool the planet.

5. Within this planetary greenhouse there are many other natural forces that distribute heat around the globe or influence the climate in other ways.

O_3 CO_2 N_2O H_2O O_3 CO_2 O_3 CH_4 CO_2

UNFORTUNATELY, THERE IS ANOTHER SIDE TO THE STORY OF THE GREENHOUSE EFFECT...

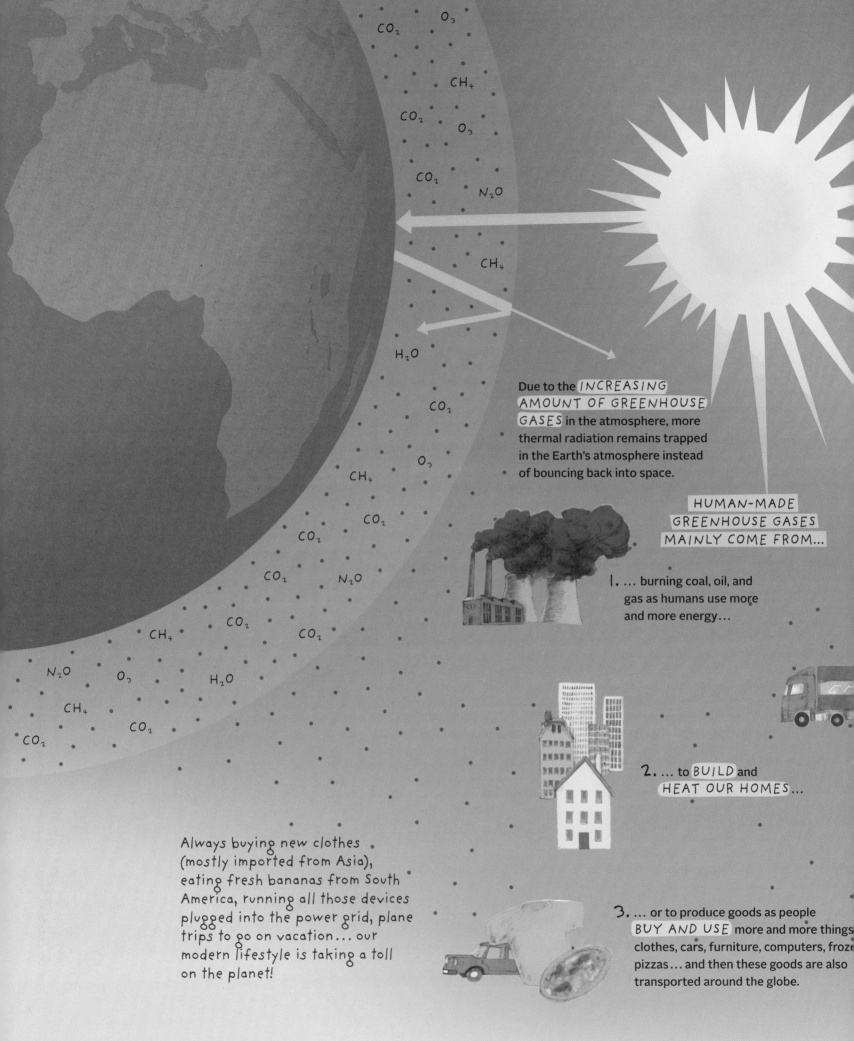

CO₂ O₃ CH₄ CO₂ O₃ CO₂ N₂O CH₄ H₂O CO₂ O₃ CH₄ CO₂ CO₂ CO₂ N₂O CO₂ CO₂ N₂O O₃ H₂O CH₄ CO₂ CO₂

Due to the *INCREASING AMOUNT OF GREENHOUSE GASES* in the atmosphere, more thermal radiation remains trapped in the Earth's atmosphere instead of bouncing back into space.

HUMAN-MADE GREENHOUSE GASES MAINLY COME FROM...

1. ... burning coal, oil, and gas as humans use more and more energy...

2. ... to BUILD and HEAT OUR HOMES...

Always buying new clothes (mostly imported from Asia), eating fresh bananas from South America, running all those devices plugged into the power grid, plane trips to go on vacation... our modern lifestyle is taking a toll on the planet!

3. ... or to produce goods as people BUY AND USE more and more things: clothes, cars, furniture, computers, froze[n] pizzas... and then these goods are also transported around the globe.

THE "BAD" GREEN-HOUSE EFFECT

The climate has changed many times during the history of the Earth (90 million years ago there was a rain forest at the South Pole—no joke!). We have been living in a warm period for around 10,000 years, which has given the world a stable and, for our taste, perfect climate, with an average temperature of 15°C (59°F). Some even suspect that it is only thanks to this warm period that people were able to invent farming and settle down, which allowed populations to grow. Unfortunately, the "bad" side of the greenhouse effect is now increasing—and that's not good news.

In 1896 another physicist, Svante Arrhenius, started to think long and hard about the climate. At that time, factory chimneys were getting rusty and dirty, because the industrial age was already relying on the burning of coal. Arrhenius realized that temperatures rise when people release large amounts of greenhouse gases into the atmosphere.

THE GREENHOUSE EFFECT CAUSED BY HUMAN ACTIVITY IS MAKING THE EARTH WARMER AND WARMER.

But it was not until the 1950s that it was possible to prove that carbon dioxide concentrations were really increasing. They have increased by more than 40 percent since the beginning of industrialization and are far higher today than at any time in the past 800,000 years. That is why we talk about the ANTHROPOGENIC GREENHOUSE EFFECT (MEANING CAUSED BY HUMAN ACTIVITY). This is added to the natural effect and leads to the climate change that we are experiencing today and that continues to get worse.

If people continue to live as we have been, if greenhouse gas emissions do not decrease, the temperatures could rise by more than 4°C (7.2°F). You will find out what this will mean to the Earth, and how we can prevent it, in part 3 of this book.

5. Many greenhouse gases also come from CUTTING DOWN AND BURNING FORESTS to use the land for pasture, or to grow crops to fatten up cattle and pigs.

This isn't smart, because the forest is a climate protector. It slows global warming by absorbing large amounts of the carbon dioxide that we humans release into the atmosphere.

4. Then there is the TRAFFIC OF GOODS AND PEOPLE on the roads, seas, and rivers, and in the air.

6. ANIMAL FARMING AND AGRICULTURE also produce greenhouse gases.

THE ARCTIC CLIMATE PUZZLE

There aren't many places left on Earth that are as unfamiliar and mysterious as the Central Arctic. There is no permanent research station out here on the sea ice. In the Antarctic (that is, at the South Pole), research is carried out at several stations throughout the year. Life is extreme there, too, but at least people have solid ground under their feet, because Antarctica is a continent, with Earth and rock under its thick layer of ice. Under the ice at the North Pole, there's nothing but cold ocean, with islands and landmasses only around the edge of the Arctic.

How are the riddles of the Arctic going to be solved? What's going on with the North Pole's climate, and why is the Arctic changing so dramatically? It will take teamwork to find out. The Arctic itself is like a puzzle that is part of the Earth's larger climate puzzle. The Arctic puzzle also consists of many parts that are closely interlinked and influence one another. The *Polarstern* researchers set out in teams to study these individual parts. Then they put the pieces together to see the big picture.

OZONE LAYER

PRECIPITATION

EXCHANGE OF HEAT AND ENERGY

ICE SHEET ON LAND

CRACK

POLARSTERN

SEA ICE FORMATION

SNOW

SEA ICE DRIFT

PERMAFROST

SEA ICE MELT

TEAM OCEAN

Studies everything that happens under the sea ice, because the sea acts like underfloor heating for the Arctic when it brings warm water from afar.

TEAM ATMOSPHERE

Focuses on everything that happens above the sea ice. It measures radiation and precipitation and records which suspended particles appear in the air and what kinds of clouds form as a result.

SUN'S RAYS

AEROSOLS (SUSPENDED PARTICLES)

AIR CHEMISTRY

CLOUDS

EXCHANGE OF GAS

PLANKTON

TEAM ICE

Explores everything to do with the sea ice and the snow on it—how ice floes form, drift, and melt.

REFLECTION FROM THE SNOW AND ICE COVER

TEAM BIOGEOCHEMISTRY

Mainly studies how gases affect the climate. Some of those gases even come from living beings!

ICE ALGAE

OCEAN VORTEX

OCEAN CURRENTS

TEAM ECOSYSTEM

Goes in search of the animals, plants, and microorganisms of this icy cold region. And it studies how they survive here.

47

WELCOME TO THE ICE CAMP

OCEAN CITY

A blue tent surrounds a large borehole in the ice. Team Ocean drops devices with sensors into the water, while Team Ecosystem gets water samples from the depths.

In front of the mighty hull of the *Polarstern*, the expedition participants set up a research camp in the middle of the sea ice. The ice breaks up again and again, piles up into ridges, and sometimes looks very different in the morning than the day before. The research teams go to work at the various stations of the camp.

ICE-THICKNESS SENSOR

DARK SECTOR

ARCTIC FOX

POLARSTERN

ELECTRICITY AND COMMUNICATION LINES

SNOW-MOBILES WITH SLEDS

ROV CITY

ICE DRILLING

CTD INSTRUMENT (to measure conductivity, temperature, and depth)

ARCTIC COD

DIVING ROBOT ("The Beast")

UNDERWATER CAMERA

MET CITY

Team Atmosphere is at work in Met City, its skyline marked by two tall meteorological towers, 11 and 30 meters (36 and 98 feet) high. Attached to them are sensitive sensors that measure things like wind speed and carbon dioxide.

DARK SECTOR

This is where Team Biogeo-chemistry collects snow and ice samples for analysis in the lab. But Team Ecosystem also works here, because they want to find out how the creatures of the Arctic survive the darkness of the polar night. The bright artificial lights of the ship could distort their research if the living beings react to the ship's light as they would to sunshine. That's why in this section it's always time for "Lights out!"

REMOTE-SENSING MEASUREMENT FIELD

Team Ice examines the floe and conducts ice drilling. Devices that look like something out of a science-fiction movie examine things like how the snow and ice surfaces reflect microwave radiation. This helps satellites measure the Arctic sea ice.

ROV CITY

The strange abbreviation ROV is short for "remotely operated vehicle," a remote-operated diving robot. From here, the expedition's robot called "the Beast" goes on risky explorations under the ice. The Beast is a jack-of-all-trades. It films the aquatic world with its camera and catches plankton for Team Ecosystem in its nets. It also examines the underside of the ice for Team Ice.

BALLOON TOWN

In the hangar tents, research balloons are waiting to be deployed by Team Atmosphere.

WEATHER BALLOONS

RESEARCH BALLOON ("Miss Piggy")

MEASURING TOWERS

LIDAR (light detection and ranging), a laser-based measuring device

CRACK IN ICE

RUNWAY FOR RESCUE PLANES

POLAR BEAR FENCE

BEAR GUARDS

REMOTE-SENSING MEASUREMENT FIELD

MET CITY

SHELTER

OCEAN CITY

BALLOON TOWN

People use snowmobiles to cross the ice between stations, but they walk as much as possible, because the exhaust from the snowmobiles pollutes the air and ice and could influence the research results.

49

IN THE (ALMOST) EVERLASTING ICE

SEA ICE IS ALWAYS IN MOTION.

Without sea ice, the Arctic would not be the Arctic. The ice stretches for thousands of kilometers/miles across the Arctic Ocean. Sometimes it lies quietly and looks like a vast snow-covered plain. At other times ocean currents and winds make the ice move. It cracks and bursts and rips apart, or it piles up into high ridges when the sea and wind press the ice pieces against each other with huge force.

SEA ICE is already special because it is made from salty seawater, so it contains a bit of salt itself. It's also a living space. There are creatures that live not only on and below the ice but right inside it. Sea ice is also constantly changing. It grows and shrinks over the years.

During the long polar night it expands until it covers a large part of the Arctic Ocean. During the summer it melts, and the ice cover retreats month by month. Seen from above, the sea ice keeps expanding and contracting—like a slowly beating heart.

At the same time, sea ice lies on the ARCTIC OCEAN like a thin skin. It separates the sea from the atmosphere, and this is what makes it such an important part of the climate system. It affects how the sea, ice, and air relate to one another, and how they exchange heat, energy, and gases. This interaction affects the climate.

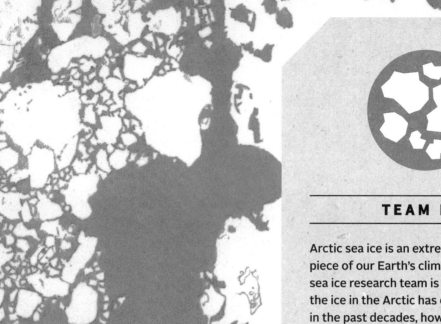

TEAM ICE

Arctic sea ice is an extremely important piece of our Earth's climate puzzle. The sea ice research team is investigating why the ice in the Arctic has changed so much in the past decades, how and when it is formed, grows, and disappears again—and what it means for the Arctic if the sea ice continues to shrink.

─── LOGBOOK ───

DATE: January 12, 2020, DAY 115

POSITION: 87° north, 108° east

TEMPERATURE: −30.4°C (−22.7°F)

Impressive! Tonight we were suddenly woken up by a strange crash. The ice outside was going crazy. The floe broke in two right in front of the *Polarstern*. Then the wind crunched the ice together, and within a few minutes there was a ridge of ice pieces taller than a baseball bat!

ALL ICE IS NOT CREATED EQUAL

Sea ice is the only type of ice that is made from the ocean water itself. It floats on the polar seas of the Arctic and Antarctic. However, sea ice does not simply form as a single ice floe on the water. It grows and changes and takes different fascinating forms, each with its own scientific name.

LOOKS YUMMY, BUT UNFORTUNATELY NOT GOOD ENOUGH TO EAT.

NILAS

When the sea is calm, the first young ice forms in a thin sheet called nilas, which if left undisturbed will continue to thicken and grow. At first it is so thin that it looks transparent, and so elastic that it bends with the ocean waves.

FRAZIL ICE

This is how sea ice is born: Tiny needles or plates of ice crystals form in the water. As more and more of it accumulates, it can turn into a cloudy soup, sometimes called ice sludge or grease ice. Ice sludge mostly forms when the water moves with the waves. If it cools down even further, it can become firmer and grow into larger ice floes.

OUR DIVING ROBOT, "THE BEAST," FOUND THIS FRAZIL ICE UNDER THE ICE FLOE.

PANCAKE ICE

This is probably the most beautiful ice. It is formed from ice sludge. As it rises and falls, the ice slush wafts back and forth on the choppy surface, forming pancake-like ice plates. The pancakes can be 30 centimeters (12 inches) to 3 meters (10 feet) in diameter. Pancake ice is more common in the Antarctic, but the *Polarstern* expedition found it in the Arctic as well.

WHEN AN ICE GIANT LIKES THIS BREAKS AWAY FROM A GLACIER, IT IS CALLED "CALVING."

ICEBERGS

Although icebergs float in the sea, they do not count as sea ice. They have broken off glaciers and consist of fresh water.

DON'T CONFUSE THIS WITH SEA ICE!

52

PRETTY TO LOOK AT, BUT IT CAN BE DANGEROUS, BECAUSE THE POOL'S ICE FLOOR CAN BE THIN. AND YOU WOULDN'T WANT TO FALL THROUGH THE BOTTOM!

MELT POND

Over the dark winter, the ice cover becomes thick and heavy. But when the sun begins to shine on the Arctic sea ice in the spring, the surface snow and the ice itself begin to melt. That's when you'll see bright blue ponds sprinkled over the ice. The darker the pond, the deeper the water. On some ice floes, whole lake districts are formed.

FINGER RAFTING

Winds and the ocean currents can press ice floes against each other. With younger ice, the pressure can produce striking shapes that look like fingers.

PACK ICE

Ships can be surrounded by what is known as pack ice. Ships get stuck in chunks of sea ice that are pushed together and on top of each other.

COLORFUL SURPRISE: A LOOK AT ICE CRYSTALS

To understand how ice grows, researchers drill an ice core from the thicker ice. Then they cut it into superthin slices—less than 0.5 millimeters (0.02 inches) thick in some cases—and examine them on a light table. By studying the crystal structure, they can tell a lot about how this piece of ice was formed.

SHELF ICE

When ice sheets or glaciers extend into the sea on land, they can form mighty ice walls. An ice shelf floats on the ocean, but is still connected to the ice sheet on the land. So an ice shelf is not true sea ice, either.

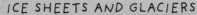

ICE SHEETS AND GLACIERS

About 90 percent of the Earth's ice is contained in the huge ice sheets of Greenland and Antarctica. These two largest glaciers in the world are land ice. While sea ice is built from salt water, glaciers are formed from snow that does not melt away in summer but instead accumulates over many years. Because these ice sheets are formed from precipitation, they are made from fresh water. Ice sheets and glaciers are the largest freshwater reservoirs on our planet!

FRAZIL? NILAS? PANCAKE? ICE IS A LOT MORE COMPLICATED THAN IT LOOKS!

FACTS ABOUT SEA ICE

IT GETS OLD AND THICK

Sea ice can live for a few years. If it hasn't lasted through a summer, it's called first-year ice. Once it has survived a summer, it is considered "old" ice. Because it melts down again and again in the summer, such ice rarely becomes thicker than 3 meters (about 10 feet), but if fragments are compressed into a ridge, it can stick up several meters or feet from the floe landscape as well as reaching ten times as deep into the ocean.

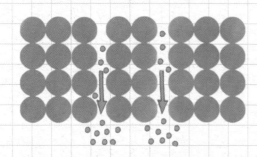

IT'S NOT AS SALTY AS SEA WATER

Compared to salty sea water, sea ice tastes sweet. This is because the sea water releases a large proportion of its salt when it freezes, and the salt sinks into the water under the ice. The older the sea ice, the less salt there is in it. However, it always contains a small amount of brine (highly concentrated salt water that is too salty to freeze). This brine forms tiny channels and pockets in the ice, which makes the ice quite porous and less hard than ice you'll find in a frozen garden pond.

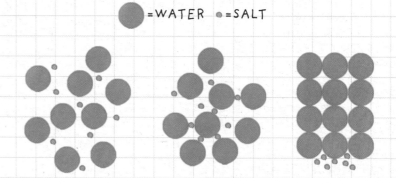

● =WATER • =SALT

CONTAINS A NATURAL ANTIFREEZE

When fresh water freezes, the water forms small crystals and becomes very rigid at 0°C (32°F). But seawater contains salt, which slows down crystallization. This means the water of the Arctic Ocean can get as cold as -1.8°C (28.8°F) before it turns into ice. The water in the Dead Sea, which contains a lot of salt, would not freeze until it was -21°C (-5.8°F).

THIS IS WHY WE SOMETIMES PUT SALT ON OUR STREETS IN WINTER TO PREVENT ICE FROM FORMING.

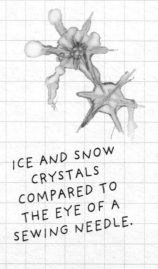

ICE AND SNOW CRYSTALS COMPARED TO THE EYE OF A SEWING NEEDLE.

PROTECTS AGAINST COOLING

When the surface of the sea touches the freezing cold air, it cools down and turns into ice. So why doesn't the whole sea eventually freeze? It's because the ice itself acts like an insulating blanket, protecting the ocean water from the colder atmosphere.

The *Polarstern* researchers use measuring sticks and ice drills, as well as sensors suspended in the ocean or air to measure the thickness of the ice and of the snow layer on top of it (the snow layer can insulate the ice from the cold air and prevent more ice from freezing).

An ice core drill is a pipe that is drilled into the ice floe. A long ice noodle about 10 cm (4 in) thick remains stuck inside, and this ice core is pulled to the surface for further study. →

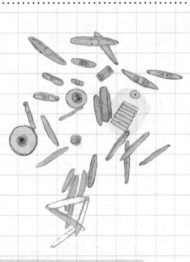

LOGBOOK

DATE: February 17, 2020, DAY 151

POSITION: 88° north, 78° east

TEMPERATURE: -33.5°C (-28.3°F)

We are surrounded by ice and snow. Even the air is full of ice crystals! Depending on the temperature and humidity, they take different sizes and shapes. Some look like solid plates or prisms. Some look like columns, stellar plates, needles, or dendrites. We make synthetic imprints so we can examine these tiny crystals closely; otherwise they would melt away under the microscope.

PROVIDES A HOME IN THE ICE

Some particularly hardy and well-adapted creatures live in the brine channels and caves in the middle of the sea ice. Bacteria, algae, worms, and tiny crustaceans come from the surrounding waters to colonize the ice and move back into the ocean when the sea ice melts again.

THE MELT

BIG

The Arctic sea ice is not just beautiful. It's an important part of our planet's cryosphere (from the Greek *kryos* meaning "cold," and *sphaira* meaning "ball" or "sphere"). The cryosphere includes all areas where there is frozen water—land and oceans that are covered with snow or ice, and glaciers, as well as the permafrost in Siberia and Alaska—ground that remains frozen year-round.

The cryosphere is as cool as it sounds, especially when it comes to our Earth's climate. Because ice and snow are light-colored, they act like a sun-protection shield for our planet. They reflect back into space some of the sun's rays that would warm the Earth if they were absorbed by it. This is especially true for the Arctic and Antarctic, where large white areas can be found. But all over the world, climate change is causing the cryosphere to disappear. Glaciers are melting. Permafrost soils are thawing out and turning to mud.

SUMMER ICE
In September, after the long summer, the ice has melted and reached its smallest extent.

NORTH POLE

GREENLAND

LOGBOOK

DATE: April 7, 2020, DAY 201

POSITION: 84° north, 14° east

TEMPERATURE: -21.6°C (-6.9°F)

Today we measured the sea ice with the ice-thickness sensor. This device looks like a torpedo attached to the end of a rope that hangs from a helicopter hovering over the sea ice. It works much like a metal detector, measuring the conductivity of the ground over which it flies. Seawater contains a lot of salt and therefore has high conductivity. Sea ice contains hardly any salt and has low conductivity. So with the help of the sensor we can distinguish between water and ice, and calculate the thickness of the sea ice.

The sea ice is also melting. You can see this most clearly from above, from the Earth's orbit. Satellite cameras have been keeping an eagle eye on the ice for decades. They can clearly measure the sea ice in September to see whether the ice has survived the Arctic summer—OR NOT.

The satellite footage is unsettling. At the beginning of the 1980s, the sea ice still extended over 7 million square kilometers (2.8 million square miles) in September. This is an area roughly the size of Australia. In September 2020, when the *Polarstern* drifted through the Arctic, the sea ice covered just 3.82 million square kilometers (1.47 million square miles). So it has almost shrunk in half!

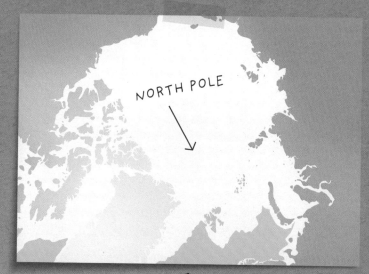

NORTH POLE

WINTER ICE
In March, after a long winter, the sea ice takes up the largest area.

RUSSIA

THIS IS ABOUT HOW FAR THE SEA ICE REACHED FROM SEPTEMBER 1981 TO 2010.

IN SEPTEMBER 2020, THE SEA ICE REACHED ONLY THIS FAR.

THINNER AND SMALLER
In the 1960s, the Arctic sea ice was still about 3 meters (9.8 feet) thick in summer. In the 1990s it was more than 2 meters (6.6 feet) thick, but in the past few years it has been less than 1 meter (3.3 feet) thick on average. So in the past four decades, the sea ice has lost about 70 percent of its volume. And here's a frightening rule of thumb: For every ton of carbon dioxide that we humans produce, about 3 square meters (32.3 square feet) of sea ice melt!

POOR CHANCES FOR SURVIVAL
In the past, a lot of ice in the Arctic survived the warmer summer months because it had been frozen solid for years, making it hard to melt. Today's ice has not been so lucky. The summers are warmer, so ice forms later in the year, does not get as thick over the course of the winter, and often does not survive its first summer melt.

LIFE ENDS IN THE NURSERY
In the shallow sea off the coast of Siberia in Russia, you can really see how early today's young ice is melting. This region is considered to be the "nursery" of sea ice—where the ice is created or "born." From here it starts its drift across the Arctic Ocean with the transpolar current. Today only 20 percent of the ice that is born off the coast of Russia makes the trip. The other 80 percent melts before it even begins its journey.

SEA ICE: A VICIOUS CYCLE

If you stand in the sunshine on a hot day, you will feel the sun's power. Its rays create warmth on Earth. If you're deciding whether to wear a white shirt or a black one on a day like this, choose the white. The white fabric will reflect—or push away—the sun's rays better, and you won't get hot as quickly as you would if you were wearing a black shirt (which will absorb the sun's rays). The same effect happens in the Arctic.

From below the water, a melt pond looks like a frosted-glass window facing the sky. The thinner the ice and the darker the pond, the warmer the water will be, which means more melting, and the bigger the pond becomes. Due to global warming, these summer ponds are melting into the ice earlier and more often.

MELT POND

Snow reflects even more solar radiation than ice. When there is a thick layer of snow on the sea ice, almost no solar energy reaches the ocean below. Over the summer months, however, the snow melts away.

SNOW

SEA ICE REFLECTS ABOUT 30 TO 40 PERCENT OF THE SUN'S RADIATION.

WARMER

COLD

When the Arctic Ocean is covered with sea ice, it's as if the ocean is wearing a white shirt. The sun shines down, and the ice reflects back a good portion of the sun's rays. This reflective power is called "albedo" (Latin for "whiteness").

Thanks to the WHITE ICE, a significant amount of solar radiation is sent straight back into space instead of warming up the Earth. Unfortunately, climate change is causing the Arctic to lose its white shirt. And not only that. Beneath the white shirt lies the dark surface of the Arctic Ocean, and like a black shirt, it warms up nicely under the glow of the summer sun.

This leads to a fatal DOMINO EFFECT. Because the sea ice is melting, it is less able to reflect the sun's rays. The solar energy stays on Earth. As a result, the atmosphere and ocean become even warmer. This has another effect on the ice, which now takes longer to freeze up in autumn. And because that means less sea ice in the coming spring, the ice will melt more quickly under the sun. And then the ocean absorbs even more heat. And so it goes. Less and less Arctic sea ice reflects less and less solar radiation back into space, sending the entire climatic system into a vicious cycle that just keeps getting warmer and warmer.

There are other effects in the Arctic that contribute to WARMING, and even scientists do not yet fully understand many of them. But they are the reason why the temperature here is rising much faster than anywhere else on Earth.

SNOW REFLECTS UP TO 90 PERCENT OF SOLAR RADIATION.

WATER REFLECTS BACK ONLY 10 PERCENT OF THE SUN'S RAYS.

When the sea ice cracks open, leads (or lanes) of ice-free ocean appear between the ice floes. The almost-black water reflects very little of the solar radiation. Instead, it absorbs more of the sun's rays and warms up.

LEAD

SEA ICE

WARM

The white sea ice prevents the ocean from heating up under the sun. But the less ice there is, the warmer the water. The warmer the water, the less ice there is...

OCEAN

59

WILL WE SOON BE IN ICE WATER UP TO ⊙OUR NECKS?

Magic trick? Nope, just physics. When the ice cube melts, the water level will be the same height that it was before.

If so much sea ice melts, won't there be more water in the ocean? As a result of global warming, the sea level has already risen, on average, more than 23 centimeters (9 inches) since the beginning of the industrial age. That doesn't sound like a lot, but if you live on the coast, it can put your cellar or even your livelihood underwater.

Rising sea levels are indeed related to melting ice. But it's not the sea ice that is to blame—at least, not directly. This is due to the special properties of water.

Most solid substances sink in water. Their molecules, the small particles that make them up, move closer together, the substance

becomes denser and the thing no longer floats on the water. But it's different when it comes to water itself. When water freezes and solidifies, it expands. Water MOLECULES move farther apart when they go from a liquid to a frozen state. That's why ice always floats. A small part, around 10 percent of the ice mass, will protrude from the water—the famous "tip of the iceberg."

If you fill a glass with water and put an ice cube in it, the cube will float, but most of it will remain underwater. If you mark the height of the water level with a line and wait until the ice cube has melted, you will see that the water level has not changed. This is because the part of the ice cube that sticks out of the water takes up the exact same amount of space as the water in the ice cube after the cube has melted.

Just like the ice cube, sea ice also floats in sea-water and takes up a certain amount of space there. The bit of ice that you see sticking out of the water contains exactly the volume that sinks into the water upon melting. When the ice melts, it turns into denser liquid water and therefore takes up less space. That's why melting sea ice has little effect on sea levels.

Unsinkable: If you throw a lump of ice into the water, no matter how hard, it will sink, but then float up to the surface again.

THIS TROPICAL ISLAND
IS DROWNING IN
GLACIER WATER.

It's different, however, with glacier ice, which sits on land, melts there, and then flows into the sea. This is what happens with the gigantic ice sheets of Greenland or the even bigger, ancient ice sheet of Antarctica. If the glaciers of Greenland were to melt completely, the world's seas would rise by around 7 meters (23 feet). If all the ice in Antarctica were to melt, too, the sea level would be around 70 meters (230 feet) higher! It's unlikely that this will happen anytime soon, but huge amounts of water are already oozing out of those giant ice sheets. In 2019, a particularly heavy year for melting, the Greenland ice sheet lost 532 billion tons of water. That's enough water to provide each of the 7.7 billion people on Earth with 190 liters (50 gallons) of water a day for a year.

The sea level is rising for another reason. Water not only takes up more space when it's frozen, but also when it gets warmer. After it reaches 4°C (39°F), for instance, fresh water expands a little with each additional degree. In the case of seawater, this happens even at lower temperatures. It's called "THERMAL EXPANSION." Because the oceans are getting warmer as a result of global warming, they are climbing up the coasts. And this is when the sea ice comes into play. When it melts, more sunlight gets into the ocean below and heats it up. And so it expands. That's why the disappearance of the Arctic sea ice also indirectly contributes to the rise in sea levels.

In fact, it's not accurate to speak of a single sea level, because due to the force of gravity, the sea level is not the same everywhere. There are regional differences, and the rise is felt more strongly in certain places. But in recent years the seas have been rising ever faster in a worrisome way. According to the Intergovernmental Panel on Climate Change (IPCC), if humans do not manage to reduce their greenhouse gas emissions, the sea level could rise by 60 to 110 centimeters (23 to 43 inches) by 2100. In Florida, 3.5 million people could be affected by rising sea levels. In Miami-Dade County alone, 90 percent of the population are affected. Worldwide, 680 million people live in flat coastal regions. Many will have to protect themselves with dykes and dams, if that is even possible. Otherwise, all they can do is flee.

190 bottles: If we tried to drink away the water that melted off Greenland in 2019, each person on Earth would have to drink this much water each day for an entire year.

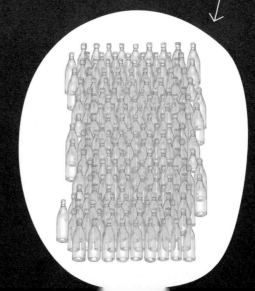

SEA LEVEL RISE UP UNTIL NOW: MORE THAN 23 CM (9 IN).

BETWEEN SEA AND SKY

In the Arctic, sometimes you can't tell the difference between up and down. When fog or snowstorms move across the sea ice, you can no longer tell where the ice ends and the sky begins. Everything is bathed in white, and the horizon disappears.

Polar researchers are afraid of weather like this, because it's dangerous for humans. Without orientation you are lost on the sea ice. Beneath you lurks the dark ocean, and the air is so cold that even your tears will freeze.

The sea ice forms a barrier between the atmosphere and the sea and prevents the two from touching. As the sea ice spreads farther and becomes thicker in autumn and winter, it becomes more and more stable. But when storms and currents pull at the ice, this protective barrier can tear open. At moments like this, the ice is amazingly loud. It cracks and crunches. Sometimes it even sounds like it is screeching.

Then something amazing happens. Through a CRACK IN THE ICE, the cold ocean water (down to -1.8°C [28.8°F]) meets the much frostier air, which can be as cold as -45°C (-49°F). That is an extreme temperature difference! Compared to the atmosphere, the sea almost seems warm. When the water comes in contact with the atmosphere, it evaporates, rising up into the air in a ghostly haze called "SEA SMOKE."

Large amounts of heat and moisture are released into the Arctic atmosphere through these cracks, which then can form more clouds. The expedition explores the enormous impact this has on the climate. Due to climate change, the sea ice has become much thinner and more fragile, even in winter. Over the course of the polar night, cracks in the ice occur much more often.

YOU WOULDN'T EXPECT TO SEE WATER VAPOR IN A PLACE THIS COLD.

← THE ARCTIC IS STEAMING.

TEAM ATMOSPHERE

Both climate and weather take place in the atmosphere. And this is where the greenhouse effect also occurs. So any changes in the air and sky will have an effect on the climate. That's why atmospheric research is a central part of climate science.

THE EARTH'S "STEAM BALL"

NORTHERN LIGHTS APPEAR AS → DIFFERENT COLORS IN THE ATMOSPHERE.

The higher you go, the thinner the atmosphere becomes. Although the Earth's gas mantle reaches 500 to 10,000 kilometers (310 to 6,210 miles) up into space (at its outermost, very thin layer), every astronaut is astonished at the sight of it. Seen from outer space, the atmosphere looks delicate and vulnerable. If the Earth were an apple, its atmosphere would only be as thick as the peel!

Translated from the Greek, "atmosphere" means something like "vapor" or "steam ball." In fact, water vapor makes up just a small amount of the gas envelope surrounding our planet. Our air consists of about 78 percent nitrogen, 21 percent oxygen, and 1 percent argon.

It also contains thousands of other GASES, including those that are of particular interest for climate research: carbon dioxide, methane, nitrous oxide, and ozone.

These gases may occur in the atmosphere in very small proportions, but they include particularly effective greenhouse gases, such as methane and carbon dioxide.

The atmosphere itself can be divided into different layers. Our weather takes place in the lowest layer, the TROPOSPHERE. This is where we find snow and rain, wind and clouds—and humans, too.

The troposphere is 12 kilometers (7.5 miles) high above the poles and up to 18 kilometers (11 miles) high at the equator. Above that lies another layer that the *Polarstern* researchers are interested in—the stratosphere.

In the stratosphere, the air is extremely cold—but not everywhere. In the lower regions it is often an icy -60°C (-76°F). Above this it becomes warmer again until temperatures reach around 0°C (32°F) about 50 kilometers (31 miles) above the Earth.

But how can that be so when we are moving closer and closer to extremely cold outer space? The answer lies in the OZONE LAYER. It sits in the middle of the stratosphere. Ozone absorbs a small amount of the radiation from sunlight and converts it into heat, raising the temperatures at these altitudes. The ozone layer also protects the Earth from dangerous UV radiation.

ATMOSPHERE

BIOSPHERE

CRYOSPHERE

LITHOSPHERE

OUR WEATHER TAKES PLACE IN THE TROPOSPHERE.

EXOSPHERE

THERMOSPHERE

MESOSPHERE

STRATOSPHERE

TROPOSPHERE

HYDROSPHERE

THE SCIENCE OF SPHERES

Because the Earth's climate system is so complex, it is easier to think of the Earth as smaller subsystems. These subsystems belong to a large, complex climate system, influence each other, and constantly interact.

The CRYOSPHERE includes all the frozen water on Earth. The HYDROSPHERE is the liquid shell of the Earth, including the oceans. The LITHOSPHERE is the solid, rocky outer layer of the Earth. And then there is the BIOSPHERE, which includes areas that are populated by living beings (plants, animals, humans, and so on).

Of all the Earth's spheres, however, the ATMOSPHERE is the one that changes the fastest. Its gases and winds sweep through the planet's gas envelope at great speed. This is what makes it so exciting for Team Atmosphere to study.

OZONE LAYER

SURPRISE OBSERVATION:
Although we have long known about the ozone hole over the Antarctic, during the expedition, a clear ozone hole formed over the Arctic for the first time, driven by climate change.

CHASING THE CLOUDS AND THE WINDS

Atmospheric researchers seek out clouds and tiny particles in the air. They measure winds, atmospheric layers, and turbulence. With the help of ultramodern technology they observe everything that lies between the surface of the ice and the ocean up to a height of more than 35 kilometers (22 miles). That's about three times higher than normal passenger planes fly.

TEAM ATMOSPHERE sets a radar trap for the wind. With its radar system, it can determine wind speeds.

RESEARCH BALLOONS regularly take off from "Balloon Town" up to a height of 35 kilometers (22 miles). They carry devices called radiosondes that analyze layers of the atmosphere to find out how cold or how humid it is in certain locations, or how the wind is blowing. Ozone sensors measure the ozone layer, and aerosol-measuring devices record the properties of dust particles.

Team Atmosphere's RADAR DEVICE works similarly to the ones police use to catch speeders. It sends out electromagnetic waves. If they hit an object such as a cloud, the waves are thrown back like an echo. The radar device picks up this echo and can tell where the object is or what its properties are, such as how much water there is in the cloud.

The biggest and most colorful balloon is called MISS PIGGY. This chubby balloon doesn't fly away like the smaller balloons because it's tied to the ground with a long rope. It can hunt aerosols, tiny suspended particles, at altitudes up to 1,500 meters (1,640 yards), and it measures radiation and turbulence in the atmosphere. However, Miss Piggy is sensitive to the weather. If the wind is too strong, the balloon stays in the hangar.

TURBULENCES ARE RANDOM CURRENTS AND EDDIES IN THE AIR.

Remote-controlled *DRONES* circle 1,000 meters (1,093 yards) above the heads of the researchers. They measure temperature, air pressure, wind, and much more.

Using *HELICOPTERS* and *PLANES* that have been adapted for extremely cold conditions, it's possible to analyze the Arctic atmosphere over large areas.

HEAT AND MOISTURE RISE FROM THE SEA THROUGH THE CRACKS IN THE ICE. THE ATMOSPHERE HERE BEHAVES VERY DIFFERENTLY THAN THE ATMOSPHERE ABOVE SOLID SEA ICE.

POLAR 5

RISKY MANEUVERS
WHITEOUT

Flying in the Arctic can be a major challenge for pilots, who dread the so-called whiteout. In fog or blowing snow, the sky and the ice-covered ground both appear white, and the horizon becomes invisible. Ice may form on the helicopter itself, which is then at risk of crashing. That's why the crew must always keep an eye on the weather.

WHY CLOUDS LEAD TO LESS ICE

CLOUD RESEARCH IN THE WILD. →

When we think of clouds, we usually think of weather. Clouds have a direct influence on whether the sun shines, whether it rains or snows. By studying the clouds and observing the sky closely, we can even predict the weather for the next day quite reliably.

Clouds are also a particularly important piece of the Earth's climate puzzle. However, simple observations are not enough, because the clouds need to be studied over long periods of time. Clouds also change as a result of climate change, because they behave differently in a warmer atmosphere. But how? Scientists use computer models to understand how clouds influence the climate. The computer makes complex predictions based on the data that is fed into it.

But this cloud data has to be collected first. And that can be complicated, because clouds are so complex. Anyone who has watched a cloud in the sky knows that it is constantly changing. Because clouds cannot be captured for study, there are even cloud laboratories in which clouds are artificially created. Another possibility is to explore them "in the wild," as scientists are doing during our expedition.

THIN ICE

SNOWFALL

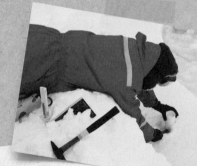

LOGBOOK

DATE: March 18, 2020, DAY 181

POSITION: 86° north, 12° east

TEMPERATURE: −30.9°C (−23.6°F)

It's fascinating to see how much insulation snow cover provides. Today we measured a layer of snow that was only 1 centimeter (0.4 inches) thick, and there was a difference in temperature of 7°C (12.6°F) between the top and bottom of the layer.

The more the climate warms
...the more cracks form in the ice
...the more water vapor rises up
...the more clouds form
...the more snow falls
...the thinner the ice becomes
...the more cracks form in the ice
...the more the climate warms
...and so on...

CLIMATE WARMING

BREAKS IN THE ICE

IS THIS ASSUMPTION CORRECT? ONLY THE DATA COLLECTED BY AN EXPEDITION LIKE OURS CAN PROVIDE PROOF.

WATER VAPOR

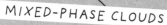

MIXED-PHASE CLOUDS

IT'S ALL BECAUSE OF CLOUDS AND SNOW

When open seawater lies beneath the freezing cold atmosphere, water vapor rises into the air and forms clouds. So the more often cracks form in the ice, the more water vapor can rise to form more clouds.

There are many different types of clouds, but MIXED-PHASE CLOUDS are special. They consist partly of frozen ice crystals and partly of liquid water droplets. These clouds can often be observed in the Arctic sky, but we don't know much about them—at least, not yet. Team Atmosphere will try to uncover their secrets in the Central Arctic.

We do know one thing. Mixed-phase clouds produce snow. Snow may be cold, but it also insulates against the cold. When a lot of snow falls, it covers the sea ice like a warming blanket and seals it off from the cold Arctic air. This means that less seawater freezes into ice. So the more snow there is, the thinner the sea ice.

The Inuit, an Indigenous group in the Arctic, have always built their igloos out of snow, because it is such a good insulator. When it is warmed up by people's body heat, the air inside the igloo can reach the pleasant temperature of 15°C (59°F).

CLOUDS ARE COMPLICATED

SOME TYPES OF CLOUDS REFLECT THE SUN'S RAYS, IN MUCH THE SAME WAY AS LIGHT-COLORED SEA ICE DOES.

Team Atmosphere also seeks out clouds to understand why the Arctic is warming up extremely quickly. Clouds have a direct influence on the temperature. However, depending on the types of clouds that form, they will cool or warm the atmosphere below them. This is just one example of their complex nature and their even more complicated effects.

In the Arctic, as in other places, when clouds roll in on a sunny day, it usually gets cooler. Like a parasol, the clouds protect the planet from solar radiation. The sun's rays reflect off the clouds before they can reach the Earth.

However, clouds can also act like a warming blanket. If the solar radiation is not blocked by clouds, it reaches the ground and warms it up. Now the ground (or the sea ice) itself releases invisible thermal radiation. If this thermal radiation is stopped by cloud cover on its way back up into space, it remains trapped in the Earth's atmosphere. Then it gets warmer— because of the clouds.

THE EFFECT CLOUDS HAVE DEPENDS ON THEIR ALTITUDE, EXTENT, AND WATER CONTENT. HERE ARE A COUPLE OF EXAMPLES.

EVERY CLOUD IS UNIQUE. AFTER ALL, EACH CLOUD EXISTS ONLY ONCE, AND USUALLY NOT FOR VERY LONG. THAT MAKES STUDYING THEM REALLY CHALLENGING.

LOW-HANGING WET CLOUDS let in less solar radiation. The air tends to be cooler below them.

FULMARS ARE TRUE FLIGHT ARTISTS. THEY GLIDE ELEGANTLY ABOVE THE WATER UNDER THE CLOUDY ARCTIC SKY.

ICE CLOUDS don't just exist in the icy Arctic, but also in our mid-latitudes. Cirrus clouds are one type of ice cloud. Some people call them feather clouds, because they look like wispy feathers floating very high in the sky. They consist of ice crystals and always seem a little disheveled because they are blown about by high winds. These thin ice clouds prevent the sun's rays from fully passing through to the Earth, but they also send hardly any heat radiation back down to the ground. So it is more likely to cool down below them.

HIGH, WET CLOUDS, on the other hand, send more heat radiation back to the ground, keeping the air warmer below the cloud cover.

THE RESEARCH AIRCRAFT POLAR 5 CAN FLY AS HIGH AS 3,000 METERS (3,281 YARDS). THIS IS WHERE MID-LEVEL CLOUDS CAN BE FOUND.

EXPERIMENT
WITH NIGHT CLOUDS

Different clouds have different effects on the climate. And things get even more complicated, because whether a cloud has a warming or cooling effect also depends very much on the region, on the season, and on the time of day. For example, cirrus clouds have a warming effect at night.

You can observe the warming influence of clouds at home, preferably at night. On a clear night, the Earth sends its thermal radiation, which it has "collected" during the day, back up into space, and the night gets cold. But if clouds are hanging in the sky, they intercept the radiation and send their own thermal radiation back toward the ground. Then the night air remains relatively mild.

In the Arctic things work a bit differently. Here, some clouds that normally bring cooling in other regions tend to bring warming. This is due to the long polar night and the low position of the sun. And we've already seen that the warmer it gets, the more cracks there are in the ice, the more water vapor gets into the atmosphere, and the more clouds there are, which results in even more warming.

71

THE BIRTH OF CLOUDS

THE TYPE OF CLOUD THAT ARISES ALSO DEPENDS ON THE TYPE OF AEROSOL.

How do clouds affect climate change? Researchers urgently need to find out. To do this, they have to understand when and why different types of clouds appear in the sky. They need to find out how clouds are born.

A cloud doesn't just appear out of nowhere. First of all, clouds need water vapor. We know that in the Arctic there is water vapor, which rises up into the atmosphere from the much warmer ocean. But even water vapor doesn't just clump up in the sky to form clouds. Something else is needed—a nucleus for the water vapor to attach to. Such cloud nuclei are provided by AEROSOL PARTICLES, which hover in the air—even in the clean Arctic air. When more and more water vapor starts to stick to an aerosol particle a droplet is formed. With more and more droplets forming, a cloud is created.

But how are these particles floating in the supposedly pure air of the Arctic? Aerosol particles are everywhere on our planet. Many are of NATURAL ORIGIN. They are formed, for example, from chemical substances that are produced by algae or plants. They can be small grains of salt that float up into the atmosphere from dried sea spray. Other tiny particles are made up of airborne bacteria, or ash from volcanic eruptions, as well as pollen, dust from windswept soil, or ash and smoke generated by wildfires burning in the tundra around the Arctic Ocean. The smaller and lighter these particles are, the farther away they can be blown by the wind; they can even fly very long distances over the Arctic Ocean.

MINERAL DUST →

SALT PARTICLE FROM THE OCEAN →

LOGBOOK

DATE: December 9, 2019, DAY 81

POSITION: 86° north, 120° east

TEMPERATURE: -24.1°C (-11.4°F)

Shooting at clouds with lasers. Our lidar devices look like something right out of a science-fiction movie. Lidar stands for "light radar," or rather laser imaging, detection, and ranging. So instead of radio waves, the lidar shoots out laser beams to hit clouds, greenhouse gases, or aerosol particles. Depending on how the laser light is reflected and scattered, we can tell how many particles there are, how big they are, and what their chemical composition is. With the help of our lidar, we discovered aerosol particles from Siberia and North America in the Arctic. We have traced them back to forest fires, desert dust, and industrial pollution. Yes, there is even air pollution at the North Pole.

⚓

Algal bloom in the Arctic Ocean. This phytoplankton produces a gas that we know as the "smell of the sea." But in the air it can become the nucleus for clouds. So algae are small cloudmakers that influence our climate.

OTHER AEROSOLS come from US HUMANS. They rise from home and factory chimneys or from the exhausts of cars or airplanes. These suspended particles often come from the same things that produce the greenhouse gas carbon dioxide! Many of these aerosols are unfortunately pretty bad for our own health. Because they are so tiny, they can get deep into our airways and cause disease. Other aerosols are released into the atmosphere as the result of massive forest fires. Most of these fires are started by humans, such as in the South American rain forest, where trees are burned down to make room for plant crops that are fed to farm animals in Europe, Asia, and North America. That means what we eat may be directly related to the burning down of rain forests and the production of aerosols. In the Arctic, however, you will mainly find suspended particles from forest fires in Canada and Siberia, where fires have become more and more common in recent years as the temperatures go up.

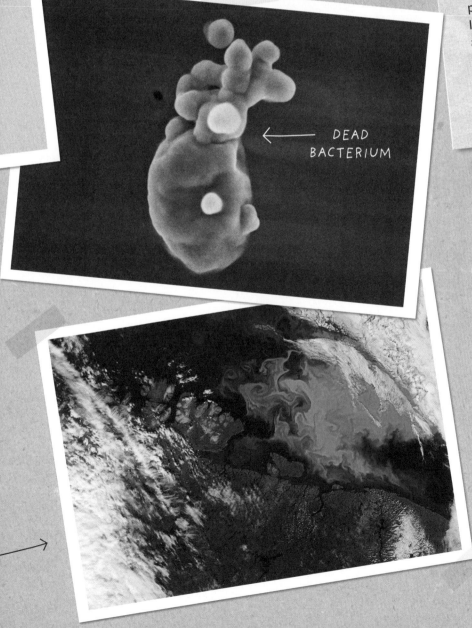

← DEAD BACTERIUM

AEROSOL PARTICLES
TINY, BUT NOT INVISIBLE

....

Aerosol particles are really tiny. Even a human hair is a hundred to a thousand times thicker. Still, you can see them. When the sky glows red in the morning or evening, this is due to the aerosols in the atmosphere. The light refracts on the particles, so that the blue and green parts are lost. If you look at a city from some distance away, you can often see the aerosols, too. Often the human-made particles collect over densely populated places as smog, making the daytime horizon look reddish brown instead of blue.

A HUGE PUZZLE FOR RESEARCHERS

In atmospheric research, there are still countless questions about the small suspended particles called aerosols. For example, what influence do they have on global warming and the climate? That is why the expedition wants to find out which aerosols are actually found in the Arctic and where they come from. Team Atmosphere chases them down with various instruments, from research balloons to laser devices. And it observes whether they create clouds, and which ones. Team Atmosphere also works closely with Team Biogeochemistry, which is studying algae—a natural source of aerosols right in the middle of the inhospitable Arctic. They are working on the theory that thanks to climate change, tiny algae called phytoplankton are thriving in the Arctic waters. This leads to more algae aerosols while at the same time more water vapor is escaping into the atmosphere through cracks in the ice. This could change the formation of clouds, and the team is closely monitoring whether these clouds then create a cooler or milder climate around the North Pole.

MYSTERIES OF THE DEEP

RESEARCH AT THE
GATEWAY TO
THE "UNDERWORLD"

NOT HOSTILE TO ALL LIFE: THE EXPEDITION EVEN ENCOUNTERS BEAUTIFUL SEA CREATURES CALLED SIPHONOPHORES.

TEAM OCEAN

Without the oceans, our Earth's climate system would look completely different. That's because the oceans store heat and transport it around the world—even to cold regions like the Arctic. At the same time, there is a great deal of interaction between the oceans and the atmosphere, because they exchange heat as well as various gases. Little was known about what was going on in the Arctic Ocean during the winter until Team Ocean came and lowered its instruments into this mysterious, black, and ice-cold underwater world.

When the *Polarstern* scientists walk across the ice camp, they sometimes almost forget that they are not actually on land. They stand on a thin sheet of sea ice, and right below lies the cold darkness of the Arctic Ocean. To explore this fascinating world beneath their feet, the men and women in the Ocean City camp have drilled a hole in the ice. They lower measuring instruments through this gateway and down into the dark depths. The Arctic Ocean can be more than 4,000 meters (4,374 yards) deep, and some devices can penetrate right to the bottom. One of them, the CTD ROSETTE, looks like large bottles tied together in a circle surrounding the heart of the CTD: instruments that measure things like the salt content and temperature of the water. The bottles also gather water samples to be examined in the ship's laboratories. To prevent the samples from freezing as soon as they hit the cold air, the tent around the ice hole is heated a little. This probably also explains why it is such a popular meeting place for all the teams in the middle of the ice camp.

THE WORLD'S OCEAN CURRENTS

NEW YORK

LONDON

GULF STREAM

A WHOLE SYSTEM OF OCEAN CURRENTS LIES BENEATH THE SURFACE OF THE SEA. THESE INCLUDE WARM (RED) AND COOL (BLUE) CURRENTS.

Through Ocean City's ice hole, researchers can access the Arctic Ocean beneath their feet. But it also gives them access to the rest of the world, because all of the Earth's oceans are connected by currents. If Team Ocean were to come across a brightly colored rubber duck at the North Pole, it would not be particularly surprising. Yes, rubber ducks.

In 1992, a container ship in the Pacific was caught in a severe storm. A container of 29,000 colorful plastic ducks, beavers, and turtles tumbled overboard and escaped to freedom. In the following years they also proved to be lucky finds for marine research. Because when they were washed ashore, whether in Chile, Australia, or Alaska, scientists learned a lot about the movement of ocean currents. Many of the plastic animals are still swimming through the world's oceans today. One of them may even have made it to the North Pole.

Ocean currents are like rivers that run through the middle of the seas. That might sound strange, but water can flow through water without mixing in too much. Masses of water not only move across the surface of the sea, but also pass each other at depths of thousands of meters/yards. They swirl around each other and rush down to the sea-floor like waterfalls. It can be like a roller coaster beneath the surface of the water.

There are several major ocean currents in the world. And they carry not only rubber ducks, but also heat, oxygen, carbon, nutrients, icebergs, and abandoned boats—as well as, unfortunately, a lot of garbage.

GARBAGE LIKE THOSE RUBBER DUCKS?

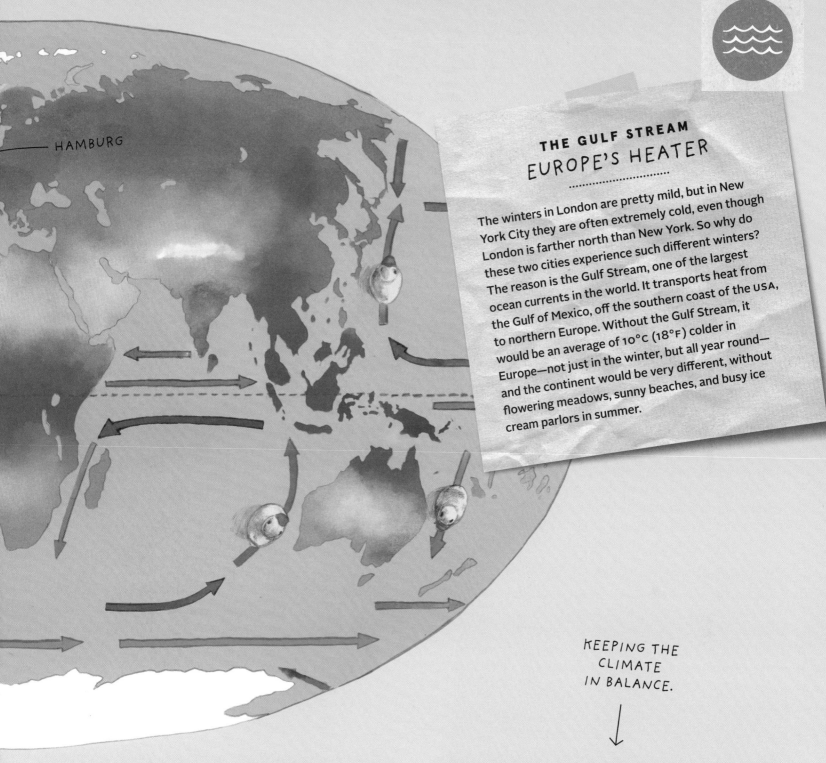

HAMBURG

The winters in London are pretty mild, but in New York City they are often extremely cold, even though London is farther north than New York. So why do these two cities experience such different winters? The reason is the Gulf Stream, one of the largest ocean currents in the world. It transports heat from the Gulf of Mexico, off the southern coast of the USA, to northern Europe. Without the Gulf Stream, it would be an average of 10°C (18°F) colder in Europe—not just in the winter, but all year round—and the continent would be very different, without flowering meadows, sunny beaches, and busy ice cream parlors in summer.

KEEPING THE
CLIMATE
IN BALANCE.

↓

Because of this massive movement of water around the planet (the great ocean currents are often called the "GLOBAL CONVEYOR BELT"), the oceans have a real influence on the Earth's climate and weather. When the hot sun shines down on the water at the equator, the sea becomes very warm there. At the poles, however, the oceans receive less heat due to the lower position of the sun, and they get no sun at all during the months of polar night. But ocean currents transport heat from the equator to the polar regions. On its long journey to the north, the seawater cools down more and more until it finally flows, refreshed from the poles, back down toward the equator.

Without the ocean-current system, the temperature difference between the regions at the poles and at the equator would be much greater. That applies not only to the water temperature, but also to the air, because the oceans and the atmosphere always trade their warmth with each other.

So we shouldn't underestimate the Arctic Ocean just because it's the smallest ocean in the world. It's less than one and a half times the size of Europe, but it acts like an AIR-CONDITIONER for the planet and plays an extremely important role in our climate system.

A SEA FULL OF SURPRISES

The Arctic Ocean is a sea unlike any other—relatively warm in the depths and almost fresh on the surface!

It's actually amazing that ice is floating on the Arctic Ocean. Because just 200 meters (218 yards) below the surface, the ocean currents bring enormous amounts of warm water from the Atlantic. They carry so much heat into the Arctic that they could theoretically melt the sea ice completely! This doesn't happen because of the particularly strong WATER STRATIFICATION in the Arctic Ocean. Water masses can not only flow past each other, but they can also lie on top of each other if they differ in temperature and salt content, which will affect their density. In the central Arctic Ocean, an upper layer of cold, fresh (that is, low-salt) water lies like a barrier between the warmer water in the depths and the sea ice that floats on the surface.

In the marine regions near Greenland, these differences in temperature and salinity drive the ocean currents. Cool, salty water is denser and therefore heavier, so it sinks, creating SUCTION that pulls in other water to take its place.

However, as a result of global warming, more and more sea ice is melting, and more fresh water flows into the sea from the land, where the glaciers are melting. This will make the Arctic Ocean less salty and, of course, warmer. This in turn could affect the circulation of ocean currents—and that brings us back to the climate.

ON THE HUNT FOR EDDIES

Sometimes patches of water break away from the great ocean currents and make their own way. They begin to spin in circles and speed through the seas. Science calls these breakaway flows "vortexes," or "EDDIES." Eddies can be a few hundred meters/yards or up to 100 kilometers (62 miles) in diameter! Similar to high- and low-pressure cells on a weather map, they can sometimes even be seen from space.

Eddies stir up the seawater, transporting and mixing warm and cold water masses in and to the Arctic. For the sea creatures who live there, they are a kind of delivery service, because they also stir up and carry important nutrients.

LOGBOOK

DATE: April 27, 2020, DAY 221

POSITION: 83° north, 15° east

TEMPERATURE: -13.6°C (7.5°F)

The "hippie" is an orange instrument with hairy threads around its "head." It dives to a depth of 400 meters (437 yards) and records how turbulent the ocean is. Last week we observed how a storm had stirred up the top 70 meters (77 yards) of the seawater.

WHO WILL GO WITH THE FLOW?

THIS INSTRUMENT MEASURES OCEAN CURRENTS. OUR BEAR VISITOR FINDS IT ALL PRETTY INTERESTING, TOO!

LINGO FOR OCEAN RESEARCHERS

The Arctic Ocean is getting warmer and more like the Atlantic. Even animals are advancing north from warmer regions. This is why one speaks of an ATLANTIFICATION of the Arctic Ocean.

Eddies carry their own kind of passport. Their composition of nutrients or trace substances reveals where they come from. Trace substances are residues of pollutants such as fertilizers or pharmaceuticals. So eddies don't just bring good things. The research team is therefore on an eddy hunt. They are taking a close look to see whether the eddies are also swirling up warm water from the depths of the Arctic Ocean and helping to melt the sea ice. This warmer water, which flows from the Atlantic into the Arctic, has become even warmer due to climate change. In addition to the eddies, Team Ocean also studies the effects of the wind. The researchers observe how violent storms are causing sea ice (and the *Polarstern* along with it) to drift across the ocean much faster. Their measuring devices show that the upper layer of water becomes thoroughly mixed in as a result, because the drifting ice pulls the water underneath along with it, bringing warmer water up from the depths and melting even more ice.

79

AS THE EARTH WARMS, SO DOES THE SEA

Svante Arrhenius was a clever man. Way back at the end of the nineteenth century, the Swedish physicist already suspected that smoking coal stoves could affect the climate. Still, climate change was underestimated for almost a century. The seas are to blame. By absorbing the consequences of climate change for so many years, they tricked us into thinking it wasn't happening.

The oceans are a gigantic STOREHOUSE OF HEAT. A large part of the heat caused by the human-created greenhouse effect does not stay in the atmosphere but is hidden in the water. The oceans have absorbed more than 93 percent of this thermal energy.

We've gotten off lightly as a result, but the warming is creating a huge mess in the oceans. For example, in the region of the Fram Strait, between Greenland and Spitsbergen, warm water (3 to 6°C [37 to 43°F]), which has been transported by the Gulf Stream through the Atlantic, flows north into the Arctic Ocean, cooling down along the way before it makes its way back south. But since the late 1990s, the water flowing into the Arctic from the Atlantic has already warmed by 1°C (1.8°F). This not only affects the Arctic climate system, but this warmer water also flows past the coast of Greenland, where it leads to the melting of the many glaciers that protrude into the sea.

GREENLAND

DRIFTING POLARSTERN

FRAM STRAIT

WARMER WATER EATS ITS WAY INTO THE GLACIERS JUTTING OUT INTO THE SEA. THE ICE SHEETS OF GREENLAND ARE MELTING SEVEN TIMES FASTER THAN THEY WERE IN THE 1990S.

ATLANTIC OCEAN

ARCTIC OCEAN

COOLED IN THE ARCTIC, OCEAN WATER FLOWS BACK SOUTH.

LIFESAVER IN THE ICY WATER
THE SURVIVAL SUIT

....

Breaking through the ice and falling into the freezing waters of the Arctic Ocean is life-threatening. That's why researchers wear special survival suits on risky missions. You may look and feel like a frog-man, but that suit will keep your body dry and buoyant, even in icy water.

SVALBARD

DISRUPTING THE OCEAN CURRENTS

For years, scientists have observed a disturbing phenomenon. The powerful Gulf Stream is getting weaker. The MELTWATER from the Greenland glaciers could be the reason. When this less-dense, lighter fresh water settles on the surface of the ocean, denser water can no longer sink into the depths so easily. The meltwater stalls an important engine that drives the conveyor belt that moves ocean currents around the world. This is why some researchers think that climate change will actually make Europe colder. The weaker the global ocean conveyor belt, the slower the Gulf Stream, which will no longer pump as much heat from the south up to the European coasts.

If the Gulf Stream stalls, it could become very cold in the U.K., Scandinavia, and Iceland. Scientists do not agree on whether a weaker GULF STREAM would really lead to such a cooling for Europe, but it would not be the first time in our planet's history. Around 10,000 years ago, the ice sheets melted, and meltwater suddenly ran into the sea. That messed up the Gulf Stream so much that temperatures fell in Europe and North America.

WARMER WATER FLOWS NORTH FROM THE ATLANTIC.

NORWAY

ACID ALERT!

Thank goodness for the oceans. Without them, we'd all be feeling the consequences of climate change even more. However, our greenhouse gas emissions are not only causing ocean temperatures to rise. There's another downside. The seawater is storing huge quantities of carbon dioxide. What does that do to the oceans?

Since industrialization began around 250 years ago, the oceans have absorbed more than a quarter of the carbon dioxide we humans have caused through traffic, deforestation, animal husbandry, industry, and so on. So far, the oceans have provided a kind of buffer against climate change. If all this carbon dioxide were in the atmosphere instead of in the oceans, global warming would have progressed much further. A big thank-you to our oceans!

But when CARBON DIOXIDE dissolves in water, it forms carbonic acid—the same stuff that tingles your tongue when your drink lemonade. The seas, however, and especially much marine life, don't like carbonic acid, because it changes the chemical equilibrium of the oceans, which have already become almost 30 percent more acidic due to carbon dioxide. Our greenhouse gas emissions not only change life on land, but also the world underwater.

↑
CARBONATED
SEAWATER

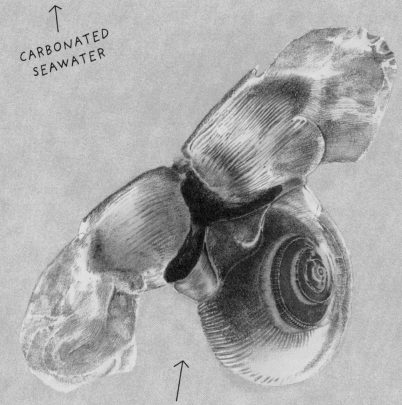

↑
SEA BUTTERFLIES
are only 0.5 to 3 millimeters
(0.02 to 0.12 inches) in size,
and they are as beautiful
as they are sensitive.

↑
THIS PROCESS IS CALLED
OCEAN ACIDIFICATION.

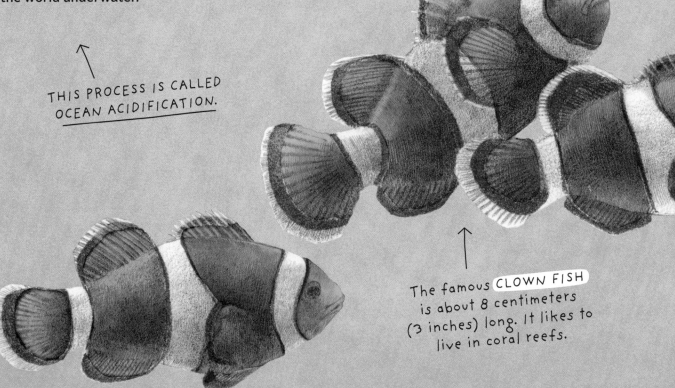

↑
The famous CLOWN FISH
is about 8 centimeters
(3 inches) long. It likes to
live in coral reefs.

CO₂ IS SOLUBLE IN COLD WATER, AND THERE IS PLENTY OF THAT IN THE ARCTIC. THIS MEANS THE POLAR SEAS ARE BEING HIT PARTICULARLY HARD BY ACIDIFICATION.

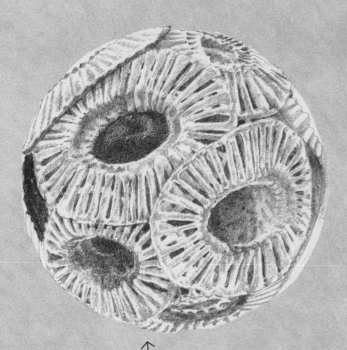

This single-celled algae is called EMILIANIA HUXLEYI, and it is so small you can't even see it without a magnifier. It floats in the seas in gigantic quantities. Its shell is formed from calcium carbonate.

NOT SO SALTY
WHAT DOES THE OCEAN TASTE LIKE NOW?

Don't worry, the ocean still tastes salty. Ocean acidification doesn't mean the water is actually turning into acid, but it will be a touch more acidic. In other words, less basic, or alkaline. Whether something is acidic or alkaline depends on the concentration of acid particles. The value is measured in pH. A pH value of 0 is super-acidic. A pH value of 14, on the other hand, is very alkaline (which is just as dangerous). The water in the ocean has had a life-friendly average pH of 8.2.

But due to human-caused greenhouse gas emissions, the pH value has dropped to 8.1. That looks like a tiny difference, but it represents an almost 30 percent increase in acidity.

By 2100, the pH of the oceans could go down to 7.7. That would make them up to 150 percent more acidic—a fatal environment for many sea creatures, because the pH value would have dropped so quickly that they would have no time to adapt.

CONFUSED FISH, RAGGEDY SEA BUTTERFLIES

Acidification is a problem for the oceans' ecosystems. Scientists have observed how orange-striped clown fish become confused in more acidic water. They will even swim toward their predators instead of getting away as quickly as possible. Young fish apparently lose their sense of smell and can no longer distinguish their parents from other animals.

Acidification is also a threat to all living things with calcium shells. If the water is too acidic, mussels and algae can no longer form enough calcium for their outer shells. The more acidic water also attacks the calcareous skeleton of coral, and when coral reefs die, a huge habitat dies with them. In the Arctic, the sea butterflies are endangered. These tiny winged snails float through the cold waters with the help of their winglike feet. In more acidic seas, it is more and more difficult to build up the calcium they need for their intricate shells. They are one of the key species that feed fish, whales, seals, waterfowl, and polar bears, as well as humans. If they are missing, there are consequences for all the creatures in the Arctic FOOD WEB.

OCEAN OR GARBAGE DUMP?

The 29,000 rubber ducks and other toys that escaped from that container ship a few decades ago told scientists a lot about ocean currents. But those ducks are not alone out there. In fact, they are in particularly bad company. In addition to the ducks, billions of tons of plastic waste slosh through the oceans.

FULMARS are particularly threatened by the plastic plague. These elegant fliers peck food from the surface of the water. Researchers have discovered dead fulmars with stomachs full of indigestible plastics. The birds starve to death with a full stomach. →

Welcome to the plastic age! Whether in our everyday life or in ditches, in meadows, and on forest paths, plastic is probably the most successful material of our time. And the problem it creates is often much more obvious than climate change. Plastic waste degrades very slowly, as it is gradually ground up by wind and water or broken down by uv radiation from the sun. This creates microscopic particles—MICROPLASTICS—that haunt the environment.

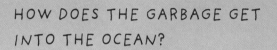

HOW DOES THE GARBAGE GET INTO THE OCEAN?

Disposable cups and cutlery, packaging, cell phones, clothing, shoes, sporting goods, fishing nets—almost everywhere we have replaced natural materials with plastic. Our lives are plastic-rich. From our closets to our refrigerators—our everyday life is full of them. Between 1976 and 2018, plastic production grew by more than 700 percent worldwide. That has ended up creating an incredible amount of garbage. Most of the plastic in the ocean comes from countries where waste is not recycled. But often it isn't the people who live in those countries that produced the garbage in the first place. It's us. To get rid of our trash, we sell it to other countries, where it is not recycled but stored at unregulated collection points. From there, the garbage ends up in nature and ultimately also in the sea.

HOW LONG DOES IT TAKE FOR GARBAGE TO BREAK DOWN INTO MICROPLASTICS?

Plastic shopping bag: 20 years
Styrofoam cup: 50 years
Plastic bottle: 450 years

EATING MICROPLASTICS— DOES IT MATTER?

Microplastics are tiny. Now there is more and more evidence that the particles can accumulate in animals until they can no longer take in sufficient food. Tests on mussels have shown that the particles settle right in the tissue, where they can cause inflammation. When living things like crabs eat the plastic, it can get into other animals that eat the crabs, and also into humans via the food web. And the plastic itself can contain harmful chemicals.

For larger animals, however, even the bigger plastic garbage is a deadly danger. Turtles, dolphins, and birds mistake the plastic pieces for food. And a plastic bag in the water doesn't just look like a jellyfish; to sea turtles, plastic waste can even smell like a nice snack, because algae settle on it. Huge amounts of plastic have also been found in the stomachs of stranded whales.

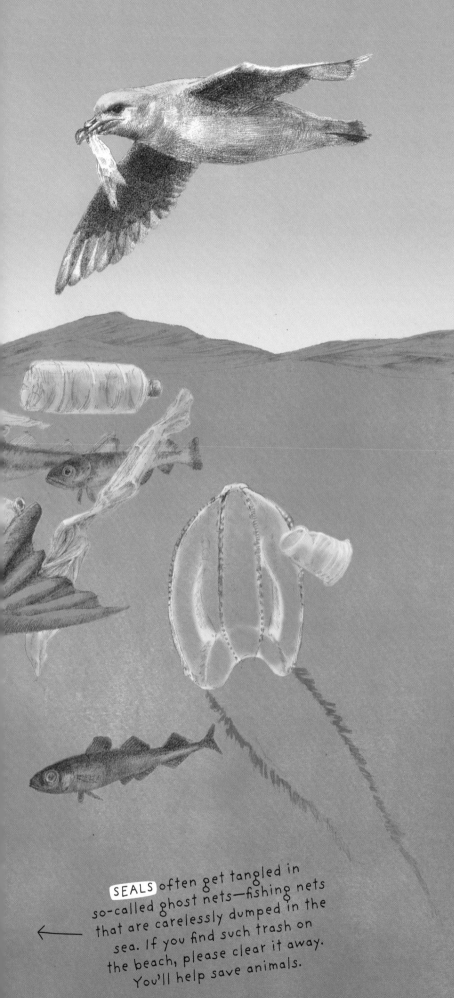

SEALS often get tangled in so-called ghost nets—fishing nets that are carelessly dumped in the sea. If you find such trash on the beach, please clear it away. You'll help save animals.

SEARCHING FOR PLASTIC AT THE NORTH POLE

GARBAGE EVERYWHERE
WHAT CAN WE DO?

A lot! Every time we take our own bag with us to go shopping, buy as little plastic as possible, or get batches of cookies from the bakery instead of shrink-wrapped ones in the supermarket, we use less plastic. Those who recycle are also helping to protect fulmars, whales, and other marine life.

Nobody knows exactly how much plastic is floating in the sea. Some estimate that more than 12 million tons end up in the oceans each year. That would be roughly one truckload of plastic per minute! Part of it collects in large gyres on the surface of the water. Much more plastic, however, is shredded into tiny particles in the seawater and sinks into the depths. Carried by the ocean currents and winds, it can travel long distances all over the world.

The *Polarstern* researchers are looking for microplastics that have even made it as far as the Arctic. One would think that this would be like looking for a plastic needle in an icy haystack, but MICROPLASTICS can now be found everywhere on our planet—in the rain, in the Earth, in animals, on glaciers, and also in sea ice. In an earlier study in the Arctic, a research team found 12,000 tiny plastic particles in a single liter (2 pints) of melted sea ice. This huge amount astonished even the researchers.

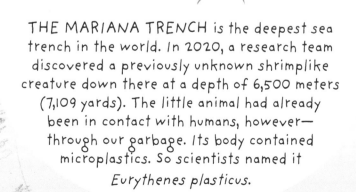

THE MARIANA TRENCH is the deepest sea trench in the world. In 2020, a research team discovered a previously unknown shrimplike creature down there at a depth of 6,500 meters (7,109 yards). The little animal had already been in contact with humans, however— through our garbage. Its body contained microplastics. So scientists named it *Eurythenes plasticus*.

PROTECTING THE FLOE

The *Polarstern* expedition takes great care to avoid polluting the ice floe and the Arctic surroundings, and to contribute as little as possible to the greenhouse effect. Nothing is thrown away on the ice. This also protects people, because "fragrant" garbage would attract polar bears. It's better to bring all your waste back to the ship every day. There the garbage is separated and either disposed of back on land or, in the case of paper or kitchen waste, incinerated on board. And the expedition has one special advantage. Although the *Polarstern* has to use energy for heating, by being carried along with the drift ice, the ship is propelled by natural power, using a truly eco-friendly method of propulsion.

LOGBOOK

DATE: November 23, 2019, DAY 65

POSITION: 85° north, 120° east

TEMPERATURE: –20.6°C (–5.1°F)

Lights out in the Dark Sector! This is where the biogeochemistry team is studying what microorganisms are doing in the ice during the polar night, because these tiny creatures can create greenhouse gases. We remove long ice cores with drills and bring them to the *Polarstern* for more detailed examination. In doing so, we have to avoid another type of pollution—light pollution. We need to make sure the Arctic organisms do not react to the artificial light and distort the research results. This is why only red light, which is less bright, may be used in the Dark Sector.

⚓

LOGBOOK

DATE: January 7, 2020, DAY 110

POSITION: 87° north, 114° east

TEMPERATURE: –29.1°C (–20.4°F)

The polar night is alive—whether with seals, cod, or plankton. Even in the dead of winter, things are lively—and creatures are nibbling on our data cables. An Arctic fox has been visiting us for days, which makes us very happy… if only it didn't have a taste for our equipment! We need to make sure it doesn't get a stomachache.

⚓

LIFE IN EXTREME CLIMATES

FULMARS

ICE ALGAE
One of the main food sources in the Arctic.

ARCTIC FOX
Often follows polar bears and feeds on their leftovers. In 2018 a female fox was tracked by GPS as it migrated across the sea ice from Europe to North America, traveling more than 3,500 kilometers (2,175 miles) in just seventy-six days!

ARCTIC COD

JELLYFISH

ARCTIC RINGED SEAL
With the help of its long claws, it can hold air holes open even in thick ice.

AMPHIPOD

COPEPOD

BELUGA

ZOOPLANKTON
These tiny animals feed on microscopic algae and other zooplankton species.

NARWHAL
The horn is actually a tusk that this "unicorn of the seas" can use like a club when hunting fish.

PHYTOPLANKTON
These microscopic algae are the zooplankton's favorite food.

CLIONE LIMACINA
This small-winged slug is also called a sea angel.

GREENLAND SHARK
The Methuselah among the vertebrates. They live to be 272 years old on average, though one specimen has been found to be almost 400 years old.

ZOOPLANKTON

POLAR
BEAR

WHO IS EATING WHO OUT THERE? MANY SPECIES IN THE ARCTIC DEPEND ON EACH OTHER—IF MAINLY AS PART OF THEIR MEAL PLAN. THERE'S NOT MUCH CHOICE WHEN IT COMES TO FOOD.

TEAM ECOSYSTEM

Months of total darkness, a landscape of drifting sea ice, and an ocean with water temperatures around the freezing point. The Central Arctic doesn't exactly look like a comfortable place to live. Yet the sea ice is full of life—on top of it, under it, and even inside of it. Before the *Polarstern* expedition, science had many unanswered questions. What do living things do in the darkness of the polar night? How many survive the winter, and which of them are also active at night? Could moonlight affect their metabolism? What does the food web look like, and who is eating whom out there? And what happens when the light returns in the spring after months of darkness?

Team Ecosystem takes a close look at the life forms in the ice and ocean to answer these questions. And answers are urgently needed. The melting of the ice and rising ocean temperatures are putting many Arctic creatures in danger. Since the Arctic is changing so dramatically, we need to understand it, so we can make the right decisions to help the polar ecosystem.

SEA ICE BIOTA
This is the name given to the many different microorganisms that live in a community inside the ice. They include bacteria, fungi, viruses, single-celled algae, and tiny multicelled animals.

WALRUS
These heavy giants live near the coasts. They have an ample layer of fat (up to 8 centimeters [3.15 inches] thick) that protects them against the cold.

BENTHOS
These animals that live on the seafloor include crustaceans, spider crabs, and worms.

BOWHEAD WHALE
It filters seawater through its baleen to catch zooplankton.

RULERS OF THE ARCTIC

← POLAR BEAR VISITS TO THE CAMP

They are almost invisible against the white backdrop of the icy landscape. Polar bears, the undisputed rulers of the Arctic, are a prime example of perfect adaptation to life in an extreme environment. Along with their close relatives from Alaska, the Kodiak bears, they are considered to be the largest land carnivores on the planet. All of us on the *Polarstern* expedition must take measures to protect ourselves from the bears when we venture deep into their realm.

If you happened to brush the fur of a polar bear (something you should of course never do!), you would be surprised. Under the white fur, the skin is dark, almost BLACK This is one thing that makes the polar bear a real expert in dealing with the cold. Strictly speaking, its hair is not white, but transparent. Sunlight shines right through each hair, reaching the dark skin, which absorbs the sun's warmth. A protective layer of fat almost 10 centimeters (4 inches) thick provides good insulation, too.

↑ ITS SCIENTIFIC NAME IS NOT "POLAR BEAR," BUT ACTUALLY TRANSLATES TO "SEA BEAR." IN FACT, THIS SEA ICE DWELLER IS CONSIDERED A MARINE ANIMAL.

CHARACTERISTICS
POLAR BEAR

SCIENTIFIC NAME
Ursus maritimus

WEIGHT
About 600 kg (1,323 lbs)

SIZE
About 2.5 m (8.2 ft) long. About 1.6 m (5.3 ft) from ground to shoulder

SPEED
About 40 km (25 mi) per hour (running)

← WHICH MEANS THAT RUNNING AWAY FROM A BEAR IS USUALLY NOT A GOOD IDEA...

ENDANGERED RULERS

Polar bears live on the Arctic coasts and on the pack ice, and they prefer to HUNT SEALS. They lie in wait for their prey at breathing holes in the floes. Polar bears usually avoid humans, but they can also be very curious!

THE BEARS OFTEN POKE AROUND THE INSTRUMENTS AND EQUIPMENT IN THE ICE CAMP.

As the rulers of the Arctic ice world, the bears have no natural enemies. Climate change, however, is a real threat. As the ice melts, their livelihood is disappearing right beneath their paws. Without the wide stretch of sea ice that has traditionally been their seal-hunting grounds between the mainland and the North Pole, the bears are stuck for longer periods on the coast, where they are driven by hunger to search human settlements and garbage dumps for food. In Siberia in 2019, fifty polar bears roamed through a village in search of food.

ABSOLUTELY ESSENTIAL
BEAR PROTECTION

The expedition is well guarded against visiting bears, both to protect the team and the animals themselves. A trip wire surrounds the ice camp. If a bear steps on it, a pyrotechnic rocket ignites, which scares off the animal with lights and hissing. On the *Polarstern* bridge, infrared cameras can observe whether an animal is approaching the camp. Bear guards accompany the science teams on the ice. Even most researchers are trained for this job. Some of the guards use helmets with night vision. If a polar bear does appear in the camp, everyone immediately retreats to the *Polarstern*.

THEIR BODY SHAPE AND FINS MAKE SEALS GREAT SWIMMERS. BUT THE POLAR BEAR ALSO HAS WEBBING BETWEEN ITS TOES.

If they have to, polar bears can go without food for months. Healthy animals can survive for two hundred days without eating. But if climate change continues unchecked, their seal-hunting season threatens to be too short for the bears to put on enough weight to survive, and even strong bears could simply starve to death.

HITCHHIKING THROUGH THE ARCTIC

HOW ARCTIC COD TRAVEL WITH THE ICE.

The little Arctic cod is a fish made for extreme conditions. It has antifreeze protection in its blood and uses the sea ice as its, well, travel vehicle. It has adapted perfectly to the environmental conditions of the Arctic Ocean. It is also one of the most important animals in the Arctic food web.

While the polar bear dominates the top of the sea ice, Arctic cod have established themselves underneath the ice cover. As youngsters, they live in the cracks and caves that run through the underside of the sea ice, where they are safer from predators.

But the Arctic cod don't just use the ice as a home. As young, they discover cracks and holes in the underside of ice floes and climb inside and are then carried across the Arctic in the DRIFTING ICE, just like the *Polarstern*.

Team Ecosystem is trying to find out how the young Arctic cod survive in the extreme conditions of the Central Arctic. The only thing that is clear so far is that in summer, the fish feed on the zooplankton that live on the underside of the sea ice or drift past in the upper water layers. At the top of the menu are tiny shrimplike creatures called amphipods.

Because they eat the tiny zooplankton and are then eaten by the larger vertebrates of the Arctic, Arctic cod are one of the most important links in the Arctic FOOD WEB.

This fish only feels comfortable when the water temperature is 0°C (32°F) or less. And it is well adapted for the cold. A biochemical substance prevents its blood from freezing in this supercold environment.

OCEAN WARMING AND ACIDIFICATION make it harder for Arctic cod to survive. Far fewer and much smaller fish larvae are hatching in the warmer, more acidic water.

LOGBOOK

DATE: February 1, 2020, DAY 135

POSITION: 87° north, 95° east

TEMPERATURE: −35.5 °C (−31.9 °F)

With our fish camera and our diving robot "the Beast," we can see a wonderful and astonishingly lively world under the sea ice. A dive would be possible but can be dangerous for people, as the ice could move at any time and trap divers underneath. Through our equipment, we can watch nimble young Arctic cod swimming back and forth past the cameras. The multitalented Beast has a net that can catch zooplankton, the small Arctic cod's favorite food. We document exactly which animal species we encounter out here. We've already spotted seals, even in the deep dark of the polar night!

⚓

SEALS THINK ARCTIC COD IS DELICIOUS!

Arctic cod live in schools and are one of the most important sources of food for seals and seabirds. So when there's a lack of Arctic cod, there is also less food for these animals, and consequently also for polar bears. By slowing climate change, we can prevent this chain of starvation.

93

THE ICY OCEAN IN BLOOM

← WHY ALGAE ARE SO IMPORTANT TO THE ARCTIC.

Never before have researchers been able to observe the creatures at the North Pole as closely as the members of the *Polarstern* expedition have. From autumn through winter to spring and summer, the researchers were right in the middle of Arctic life. They could see exactly how all this life was affected— by the sea ice as it contracted or expanded, depending on the season, and by the sunlight that either bathes the Arctic in bright light or disappears completely for months at a time.

Arctic sea ice is not like a solid ice cube. It's more like Swiss cheese, full of small salty pockets and channels. And inside these spaces, as well as on the underside of the ice and in the depths of the water, live the food that sustains all living things in the Arctic: ALGAE.

Most of these algae are microscopic single-celled organisms. Research makes a precise distinction between those that live in the sea ice, called ICE ALGAE (no surprise!), and those that live in the water, the PHYTOPLANKTON. So far, more than a thousand different types have been found in the Arctic Ocean.

Algae also need LIGHT. Only then can they photosynthesize and multiply, which is what they are busy doing every spring. As the sun slowly ventures up over the horizon again, and more and more light falls—first on the ice cover and finally, when it has melted, into the water— life explodes in the middle of the ice world. This amazing spectacle is called ALGAL BLOOM. The small plants then cover the undersides of the floes in green-brown carpets, and the melt pools on the surface of the ice shine a beautiful turquoise.

— LOGBOOK —

DATE: February 21, 2020, DAY 155

POSITION: 88° north, 66° east

TEMPERATURE: -22.6°C (-8.7°F)

Fridtjof Nansen wrote 126 years ago that his expedition had caught small crustaceans "which were so strongly phosphorescent that the contents of the net looked like glowing coals." Today we also caught a copepod that glows bluish. This fascinating creature is called *Metridia longa*.

⚓

COPEPODS

ARCTIC COD HUNTING ZOOPLANKTON

For the animal members of the plankton—ZOOPLANKTON—the table is also set. Millimeter-sized (0.04-inch) crustaceans begin to feed through the algal blooms. They themselves are a good food source for Arctic cod or even larger animals such as the bowhead whale. All of these types of plankton may be tiny, but their role in the oceans is huge. However, ice algae are particularly important in the Arctic. They provide the animals at the North Pole with half of the basic biomass in the food web. By constantly delivering this main course to all the animals of the Arctic, the sea ice becomes not only a refrigerator for the climate, but also a refrigerator for the ecosystem.

WHEN IT COMES TO FOOD, IS IT A CHAIN OR A WEB?

Different living beings are often linked to one another through their diet. A plant is eaten by a herbivore, which in turn may serve as food for a carnivore, and so on. This link is often referred to as the "food chain." But nature is more complex than this. A herbivore usually eats not just one, but several plant species. A predator generally not only hunts various animals, but may also eat plants. Which means that so-called chain is more like a tightly interwoven food web. Because there are fewer animals and plants in the Arctic, they are all more interdependent—and the entire food web is much more vulnerable if something changes—for example, if a plant or animal species becomes less abundant.

AMPHIPODS

PHYTOPLANKTON ARE TINY PLANTS. ZOOPLANKTON ARE TINY CREATURES.

SEA SNAILS (WITH AND WITHOUT "HOUSES").

SUPERHEROES OF THE OCEAN

Team Ecosystem isn't the only *Polarstern* team interested in the Arctic Ocean algae. The biogeochemistry scientists are also taking a close look at these microorganisms—or rather, they're looking at what they produce. This is because living things—everything from people and animals to plants and microorganisms—are among the most important gas producers on the planet.

But while we humans are the main producers of the CO_2 that is damaging the climate, the most powerful gas producers in the Arctic—the microscopic algae, or PHYTOPLANKTON—have other talents. In fact, we should consider them the true superheroes of the oceans for several reasons.

Phytoplankton include diatoms, flagellates, and other strange-looking mini marine plants. And although they may be small, there are lots of them. Along with the small animal organisms called zooplankton, phytoplankton make up almost 98 percent of the biomass in the oceans: the mass of all living and dead organisms. They serve as food for fish, whales, and countless other animals: they are the basis of the ocean's FOOD WEB. Without these tiny creatures, the oceans would be nothing more than a salty, lifeless broth.

WE OWE EVERY SECOND BREATH WE TAKE TO THE ALGAE IN THE SEAS! (READ ON TO FIND OUT WHY.)

TEAM BIOGEOCHEMISTRY

The biogeochemistry team has the most finicky name of the expedition. As its name suggests, the team's work includes biology, chemistry, and geosciences, and they are doing some exciting research—tracking gases that have an impact on the climate. Biogeochemistry is particularly interested in trace gases, which occur only in small quantities but have a significant impact on the Earth, especially when they act as greenhouse gases that can cause climate change.

The Arctic sea ice acts like a lid that determines how much of these gases get from the ocean into the atmosphere and vice versa. The gases may even be hidden in the sea ice itself. The biogeochemistry team tracks down the trace gases and evaluates snow, ice, and water samples to understand the gas exchange between sea, ice, and atmosphere.

But getting back to the subject of gas. Here, too, the phytoplankton are busy. If sunlight falls on the algae, they develop a huge appetite for the greenhouse gas carbon dioxide. They then use this CO_2 for photosynthesis in order to multiply on a massive scale. This is good news for us, because through photosynthesis, these tiny things take carbon dioxide and turn it into oxygen—about half of the oxygen in the Earth's atmosphere. So here in the Arctic it is the sea, rather than the forests, that are creating the air we breathe. (Forests often get most of the credit when it comes to creating oxygen!) And it gets even better, because the algae are also an important part of the so-called biological carbon pump in the sea. When they die, they sink down into the depths of the ocean, taking some of the CO_2 that they have absorbed with them. And that literally sinks the greenhouse gas, which is good for the climate.

Phytoplankton may be tiny, but they have a huge influence. So it's cause for worry that in most of the world's oceans their numbers are falling drastically, probably as a result of climate change. But this isn't happening in the Arctic Ocean, where the light-loving plankton feel right at home as the sea ice retreats. And what this plankton "leaves behind" can be measured and analyzed by Team Biogeochemistry, which is researching another gas that arises from the algae. If you have ever been to the coast, you will recognize it as the smell of the sea. And you can find out what this fragrant algae gas has to do with the climate from Team Atmosphere (see page 72).

THE BIG THAW

Most of the talk about climate change centers on carbon dioxide. But there are other greenhouse gases, too. Methane is a particularly powerful one. It occurs in quite small doses, but it's about thirty times more harmful to the climate than CO_2. Unfortunately, climate change is causing more and more methane to enter our atmosphere.

Sea ice is like a floating freezer. Gases and other chemical substances can be stored in it, including greenhouse gases. It isn't yet clear whether sea ice is more of a source of greenhouse gases or a sink—where CO_2 is absorbed—but it is a place where climate-damaging gases can be locked in and prevented from having a harmful effect in the environment. The ocean also acts as a carbon SINK when, with the help of phytoplankton, CO_2 disappears into its depths.

But back to methane. Worldwide it is most concentrated in the atmosphere at the North Pole. So is there an unknown source out there? Even a sink that is not able to hold its METHANE anymore and is now releasing this strong greenhouse gas into the atmosphere? This is one of the big questions that the biogeochemistry team is investigating. And it has a hunch. The methane could be traveling into the Central Arctic with the sea ice—taking the same route as the *Polarstern*.

MICROBIAL LEFTOVERS

But let's take another step back—into the mud. Methane is produced when organic matter dies and decomposes. Factory farming and landfills are major sources of methane. However, anyone who thinks of methane as a stinky gas is wrong. Despite the fact that it is produced by dead things, it is completely odorless. The largest natural sources of this greenhouse gas are on the edge of the Arctic, such as in Canada and Siberia. This is where great thawing is beginning in the permafrost. By definition, PERMAFROST SOILS are frozen year-round. They can reach an impressive 1.6 kilometers (1 mile) deep in the Arctic. A quarter of the land area in the northern hemisphere has remained frozen in this way. But now this ground is turning into mud and slush due to global warming. And soil, plant, and animal remains that had previously been in deep-freeze are thawing out as well, providing a feast for microorganisms to eat; then they release methane. Some of this methane reaches the Arctic Ocean via rivers and dissolves there in the seawater. Some, however, is trapped in the sea ice and then drifts through the Arctic with the ice, just like the *Polarstern*. It's now important to find out how much methane remains trapped in the sea ice and how much escapes into the atmosphere. Especially since more and more ice is melting.

FIRE NOT FROST

Not all methane is coming from the permafrost downriver into the Arctic Ocean. Some of the greenhouse gas takes a more direct route and goes straight into the air to increase the GREENHOUSE EFFECT. And that is now leading to serious consequences on the edge of the Arctic, where many people live. In June 2020, when the *Polarstern* team was looking for methane in the sea ice, a gigantic heat wave developed in Siberia, the region with the most permafrost in the world. In the northern Russian city of Verkhoyansk, known for its cold winters, the temperature rose to a record 38°C (100.4°F)! From January to May 2020, the average temperature in some regions of Siberia was 8°C (14.4°F) above the usual mean. And as in 2019, huge areas of the Siberian forests went up in flames. These are called ZOMBIE FIRES because they "hibernate" underground, only to break out again in spring. That's a scary side of climate change. People who live in the permafrost areas are also affected when the thawing ground gives way, because roads sink, and houses and oil pipelines are damaged. In June 2020 one of the worst oil disasters in Russia occurred when a huge ramshackle diesel storage tank in a Siberian industrial plant leaked, and tens of thousands of liters/quarts of diesel spilled into the ground and poisoned the river waters.

OUR ARCTIC, OUR FUTURE

← THE ICE WORLD IS IN DANGER, BUT IF WE SAVE THE ICE, WE WILL HELP OURSELVES, TOO!

As the expedition year progresses, one thing is certain. The daring drift plan has succeeded. The *Polarstern* is still surrounded by ice, but the weather is gradually getting warmer. Summer is coming, and people on board are getting ready to say goodbye to the Arctic.

SAYING GOODBYE FOREVER?

Many of the researchers are worried. Studies show that the polar sea ice will disappear almost completely during the summer months if climate change continues unchecked, which means the North Pole would no longer be covered by ice in the summer. This could even happen before <u>2050</u>!

2050?!

THAT WOULD BE THIRTY YEARS AFTER THE *POLARSTERN* EXPEDITION. NOT A LONG TIME FOR THE EARTH.

IT'S FIVE TO TWELVE! BUT THERE IS ALSO REASON FOR HOPE. →

If the sea ice disappears, you will be able to sail a boat from the North Sea directly to the North Pole in summer. A trip that once cost many sailors not only their ship but also their lives would become a simple sailing excursion. But that would mean no polar bears or Arctic foxes would roam the North Pole. The Arctic (polar) cod would no longer travel with the sea ice, and the ice algae would no longer bloom to feed the Arctic ecosystem. And there would no longer be a bright ice surface reflecting the sunlight like a giant shield, protecting the ocean from even more warming. The Arctic climate puzzle would be in complete disarray, and this would change the Earth's climate system even more.

Fridtjof Nansen did not make it to the geographic North Pole on his drift expedition. The *Polarstern* came closer in winter than any other ship. When the increasingly fragile ice finally released the ship in summer, we made a decision. The expedition would set out to reach the North Pole after all.

SUMMERS WITHOUT ICE? NOT ON OUR WATCH!

WE MAY BE THE LAST GENERATION TO EXPERIENCE AN ARCTIC COVERED BY SEA ICE YEAR-ROUND.

But the good news is that it's now up to us whether and how often these ice-free summers will happen. The future of the Arctic depends on whether humanity lowers its greenhouse gas emissions.

IN JUST A FEW DECADES,
A DINGHY COULD SAIL FROM LONDON
TO THE NORTH POLE.
CAN YOU IMAGINE THAT?

NOTES FROM THIN ICE

⚓

DATE: March 12, 2020, DAY 175

POSITION: 87° north, 21° east

TEMPERATURE: -27.1°C (-16.8°F)

Today the sun rose above the horizon for the first time since we last saw it on October 5! We are excited to see how the ecosystem will react to the arrival of polar day, and what happens as more and more sun reaches the sea ice. After months of traveling through the polar night, the *Polarstern* will soon be drifting under the never-setting midnight sun, through the spring and summer. Where once only darkness reigned, now the light bathes the ice and turns it glistening white. We'll have to swap our night-equipment headlamps for sunglasses.

THE *POLARSTERN* DRIFTED THROUGH THE POLAR NIGHT FOR 159 DAYS WITHOUT EVER SEEING THE SUN.

DATE: April 23, 2020, DAY 217

POSITION: 84° north, 16° east

TEMPERATURE: -16.6°C (2.1°F)

A springlike warm spell has made us and the ice floe sweat profusely over the past few days. Within just a week, the temperature went from almost -30°C (-22°F) up to over -2°C (28°F), then back down to -20°C (-4°F), until the thermometer finally cracked the freezing mark.

DATE: May 10, 2020, DAY 234

POSITION: 83° North, 13° East

TEMPERATURE: -15.8°C (3.6°F)

Our ice floe is getting very restless. Cracks and leads are forming again in the middle of the ice camp. We often have to use kayaks to get to our individual research stations.

OUR EXPEDITION IS COMING TO AN END. SOME FINAL NUMBERS:

During the year, 442 people were with us on the expedition. In addition, hundreds of people come on board the supply ships and worked as support staff on land!

The members of our research team represent 37 different nationalities!

We drilled more than 1,000 ice cores.

Our research balloons went up 1,550 times.

Our robot "the Beast" dived under the ice on 84 days.

The expedition collected more than 150 terabytes of data.

We ate 6,000 kilos (13,228 pounds) of potatoes during the expedition. And tons of other provisions.

~~~~~~

After the strenuous days in the ice, we rewarded ourselves with 3,500 chocolate and candy bars.

~~~~~~

We had a supply of more than 7,700 rolls of toilet paper.

DATE: May 14, 2020, DAY 269

POSITION: 82° north, 7° east

TEMPERATURE: -2.8°C (27°F)

Last night a female polar bear came by with her little cub. The two looked curiously at the *Polarstern*, and we watched the bears from the safety of the ship. Due to the dwindling sea ice, the bears face an uncertain future. Hopefully they will still have a good, long polar-bear life.

DATE: June 23, 2020, DAY 278

POSITION: 81° north, 9° east

TEMPERATURE: 0.4°C (32.7°F)

We are in the middle of the melt season. The remaining snow is very soft and sticky. Goodbye, snow boots! It's time to get out the rubber boots.

The *Polarstern* has drifted with the ice for a total of 3,400 kilometers (2,113 miles), in many loops and circles. That's about the same distance as from Chicago to Los Angeles!

The *Polarstern* traveled 1,500 kilometers (932 miles) from the nearest human settlement.

On some days when the winds were strong, the ship drifted up to 25 kilometers (15.5 miles).

DATE: July 31, 2020, DAY 316

POSITION: 79° north, 2° east

TEMPERATURE: 2°C (35.6°F)

What a racket! Our ice floe broke up yesterday. We had just started to dismantle our research camp the day before. A good decision as it turned out. We drifted with our floe for exactly three hundred days, to the edge of the ice near Greenland, in the Fram Strait. The remnants of the floe will now drift out into the open ocean and melt. We're a little sad to see that our temporary ice home has reached the end of its life cycle. Now we're going to head back north to find out how young ice freezes at the end of summer. To do this, we'll look for a new floe.

DRIFT BEGINS

NORTH POLE

GREENLAND

THE *POLARSTERN'S* ROUTE THROUGH THE ARCTIC.

START IN TROMSØ

POSITION ON JULY 31, 2020.

POOL PARTY AT THE NORTH POLE

During our year in the ice, the *Polarstern* crew has been able to collect a gigantic treasure trove of climate data. But when the icebreaker made a detour to the geographic North Pole in August, the researchers could hardly believe their eyes.

— LOGBOOK —

DATE: August 19, 2020, DAY 335

POSITION: 90° north

TEMPERATURE: -0.2°C (31.6°F)

WE'RE AT THE NORTH POLE!

And after only six days of travel! In the past, the area that we had to cross was notorious for its thick ice, some of which was several years old—an area ships wanted to stay away from. But in front of us lay vast expanses of open ocean. Often the open water reached straight to the horizon. Our experienced captain called the situation historic. Over the following weeks we will observe how the ice develops as autumn approaches. And then we will finally leave again, but this time we'll be heading home. We are expected in Bremerhaven on October 12, 2020, after thirteen adventurous months in the Arctic.

⚓

THE POLARSTERN HEADING TO THE NORTH POLE.

"We watched the ice die. In summer it was melting heavily right at the North Pole. If we don't fight global warming immediately, the Arctic ice will soon be gone in summer." — EXPEDITION LEADER MARKUS REX

HIS FUTURE LOOKS BLEAK...

... if we humans carry on as we have been. Because with every ton of carbon dioxide that we release into the air, more ice melts away. If we continue to emit even more greenhouse gases, the Earth could warm up by as much as 4.8°C (8.6°F) by the year 2100. With the previous increase it would then be about 5.8°C (10.4°F) warmer than before the beginning of industrialization! This warming would be greater than anything we've seen since humans first existed on Earth. It would be unique on our planet for millions of years. It's not just the wonderful ice world—home to so many creatures—that needs our help, but the entire planet.

No wonder the North Pole is melting. The *Polarstern* measured temperatures in winter that were almost continuously about 10°C (18°F) higher than they were during Nansen's expedition 125 years ago!

IF WE DON'T STOP CLIMATE CHANGE, THE WORLD WILL BE UPSIDE DOWN.

7. And for those people who are already poor, things will get even worse. Droughts and floods can lead to crop shortages and FAMINE, especially in developing countries. More and more people will flee their homes due to climate impact, environmental damage, and related social crises. As they search for new places to live, there is a risk of major CONFLICTS. Climate protection can help these people.

6. So long, polar bears and friends. Because climate change is occurring at such a fast speed, animals and plants cannot adapt. There is a threat of massive species EXTINCTION.

5. SEA LEVELS will continue to RISE, which means that cities and entire regions, such as New York City, are threatened by flooding.

4. Speaking of WATER SHORTAGES, in general, as a result of droughts and floods caused by climate change, billions of people could no longer have access to clean drinking water.

3. Winter sports? In many places they could soon be a thing of the past. Alpine GLACIERS have already shrunk by half, and they will continue to MELT. Once they are gone, many regions will also suffer from water shortages.

2. Climate change can make you sick. With new climatic conditions come new DISEASES and parasites. For example, ticks that transmit dangerous pathogens are now being found in places they weren't able to survive in before.

1. WEATHER EXTREMES are becoming more and more common. We can already see this with heat waves. In 2003 the so-called summer of the century claimed 70,000 lives in Europe.

COMPETING FOR POLE POSITION

Not everyone thinks it's a bad thing that the sea ice is receding. Some even think there's an advantage to climate change. A region that was once inaccessible because of its ice is now open for business.

SHIPPING The shortest sea route between the Atlantic and the Pacific could eventually go directly through the Arctic. For the global economy, this means moving goods faster and more cheaply, which will probably lead to more people buying more things.

TOURISM A few years ago a large cruise ship traveled the Northwest Passage through the Arctic for the first time. More and more people want to see the untouched polar region.

FISHING With so much of the world's seas being overfished, the deep-sea fishing industry wants to penetrate the largely untouched Arctic fishing grounds.

RAW MATERIALS It's said that more than 20 percent of the Earth's remaining fossil fuels are in the Arctic. Such oil and gas deposits are tempting to mining companies—even if these raw materials are actually part of the problem, because it is their use that is driving climate change.

TOURISTS COMING IN EVER LARGER FLOCKS WILL ENDANGER THE PRISTINE NATURAL WORLD THAT IS ATTRACTING THEM IN THE FIRST PLACE. IT'S A PARADOX, NO?

The cold Arctic is in hot demand. In 2007, a Russian expedition rammed a Russian flag into the seabed at the North Pole. China is already planning a "polar silk road" as a trade route through the Arctic. And in 2019, U.S. president Donald Trump wanted to buy all of Greenland from Denmark. (They gave him a clear no!)

UNDERWATER BATTLEGROUND

The battle for the Arctic is literally fought on the backbone of the Arctic—namely the LOMONOSOV RIDGE, an underwater mountain range. It stretches across the Central Arctic and also runs right over the North Pole.

Millions of years ago, the Lomonosov Ridge was part of a continent, before it broke off and drifted away. If a country can prove that the seabed belongs geologically to its mainland, it can make a claim to own it. Denmark, Canada, and Russia are now each saying:

IT BELONGS TO US.

So the underwater mountain range has become a matter of dispute. Whoever owns it owns the North Pole.

WHO OWNS THE ARCTIC?

THE CENTRAL ARCTIC IS INTERNATIONAL WATERS

AT LEAST, NOT YET.
↓

IT DOESN'T BELONG TO ANYONE.

In the seventeenth century, the idea was established that there were both territorial and international waters, and that everyone had a right to sail through international zones. A "3-mile limit" applied to territorial waters (3 miles is approximately 5 kilometers, the farthest distance that cannonballs could fly). No foreign ship was allowed to enter this zone off the coast of any country.

By the late twentieth century, cannonballs had become less important, but claims to ownership of the sea increased. In 1982, countries agreed that they each had a right to 200 nautical miles, about 370 kilometers (230 miles) beyond their coastlines. This regulation applies to all oceans, including the Arctic. Countries can fish or salvage mineral resources within this area. So far, this has been of little interest in the Arctic because of the ice cover.

But things are different today. Many new opportunities to make money—and a lot of it—are sparking conflict and competition between countries as the Arctic becomes less icy and more profitable, and as different nations claim sovereignty over its open waters.

OUR ARCTIC

GOOD REASONS TO KEEP WATCH

The outlook for the Arctic economy is good. But economic arguments are not everything. There are very good reasons to stop large numbers of cargo ships, passenger cruisers, fishing trawlers, and oil-drilling companies from coming to the Arctic.

IF IT SMELLS LIKE AN OIL SPILL...

Oil spills often occur during shipping, and they are hard to clean up. Should a ship have an accident in the Arctic, an oil spill so far off the beaten track would be even more difficult to fight.

THE OCEAN AS TOILET

Too often ships dump garbage and sewage into the sea, including chemicals and plastic. Tourist cruise ships do the same, making them big-time polluters.

STRAIGHT INTO THE WHALES' EARS

Ships and underwater mining make a lot of noise. Noise travels much more easily through water than it does through the air. Marine mammals in particular can even get sick because of it. Noise-plagued whales may die after they lose their bearings and become stranded.

BLACK LAYER ON WHITE ICE

A dirty, yellow-gray cloud of exhaust often hangs over ships. Large ships run on heavy fuel oil, a poisonous waste product from oil refiners (the *Polarstern* doesn't, by the way, she runs on special Arctic diesel fuel). Although heavy fuel oil could be banned in shipping in the Arctic from 2024, there are ways of getting around this ban. And ships that use other fuels also emit huge amounts of CO_2 and soot particles. When the soot settles on the remaining sea ice, the once-white surface can no longer reflect as much solar radiation.

IT WOULD BE WISER TO JUST LEAVE THESE RAW MATERIALS WHERE THEY ARE. THAT WOULD BE BEST—FOR THE ARCTIC AND FOR THE CLIMATE.

NO CONSULTATION

No one knows the exact figures, but of the 4 million people in the Arctic, it is estimated that around 1 million people belong to distinct Indigenous groups. For example, the Inuit live in Greenland and Canada, the Athabaskans in Canada and Alaska, the Yupik in Alaska, and the Nenets in Russia. And they have been doing so for a very long time. Their traditional knowledge, interest, and opinions on the industrial use of their homeland are just as diverse. However, Indigenous people's perspectives often (and unfairly) play only a minor role in economic and political decisions.

WHAT ABOUT THE RAW MATERIALS?

Humans triggered climate change by burning fossil fuels. It is precisely these fuels, oil and natural gas, that are now to be mined again in the Arctic. And then the use of these raw materials, which have only become accessible through climate change, will create even more dramatic climate change, increasing the destruction of the Arctic. Isn't that a ridiculous idea? If you came up with this answer on a class test, you would get a big fat zero for failing to understand the problem in the first place!

RULES AROUND THE NORTH POLE

Fortunately, Arctic countries have also come up with rules to protect this beautiful and fragile landscape. Various organizations are working to make sure that, on the one hand, the interests of the 4 million people living in the Arctic are protected, while on the other hand, nature does not have to suffer because of economic development. The Arctic Council, for instance, takes into account the concerns of the different Arctic governments as well as those of the Indigenous populations. There is even a special Polar Code to make sure ships operate safely in polar waters. And in 2018 an agreement was reached by many countries to ban commercial fishing until more is known about the sensitive nature and consequences of fishing in the North Pole region.

THESE MEASURES ARE IMPORTANT. BUT INSTITUTIONS AND AGREEMENTS ALONE WILL NOT SAVE THE ARCTIC. THAT'S UP TO EACH ONE OF US.

WE WANT YOU!

FOR THE BIGGEST ARCTIC RESCUE MISSION OF ALL TIME.

So let's be clear. The climate is in a bad state. And soon the Arctic will be, too—if everyone continues as before.

BUT SOMETHING IS CHANGING.

Most people don't know much about the Arctic. But now more and more people are realizing that climate change is already a huge problem for the Earth. The changes in climate will directly affect our lives and THOSE OF THE PEOPLE WE LOVE. And it will affect the lives of our children and future generations.

The *Polarstern* brings home the missing piece of the climate system puzzle—the data from the Arctic. Thanks to the new findings, scientists around the world will better understand what the changes in the Arctic mean for the rest of the planet. With the help of better climate predictions, politicians can also make better decisions: for climate protection, for the Arctic, and for the entire Earth.

YOUR PICTURE GOES HERE.

BUT WE CAN ONLY SAVE THE ARCTIC AND THE EARTH'S CLIMATE TOGETHER.

THAT'S BALONEY!

SAVE THE PLANET

WOULDN'T THE BIGGEST DANGER BE IF WE ALL COUNTED ON SOMEONE ELSE TO SAVE THE ARCTIC

THERE'S NO POINT!
~~ONE IS NONE!~~

Some people say, "One person can't make a difference!" But if many individuals together can make a difference, then each individual must have some impact. That's only logical, right?

THAT'S WHY THE ARCTIC NEEDS YOU, TOO.

ARCTIC PROTECTION FORMULA

Getting <u>started</u> is always the hardest part. But there is a trick to it. Start with small steps, and don't try to do too much at once.

THE ARCTIC AND CLIMATE PROTECTION FORMULA GOES LIKE THIS:
WE HAVE TO REDUCE OUR ECOLOGICAL FOOTPRINT.

BUT HOW?
— produce less CO_2
— generate less waste
+ consume only what we really need
+ think more about what's good for us and for the planet

= STEPS TO SAVE THE CLIMATE

IT MAY SOUND COMPLICATED, BUT IN FACT THERE ARE THINGS WE CAN DO FOR THE CLIMATE EVERY SINGLE DAY.

HOW DO WE IMPLEMENT THIS FORMULA?

By making decisions every day—both for the Arctic and for the climate.

Our everyday life is full of decisions. Some of them are easy; others need a good dose of courage. Making decisions to protect the climate can be particularly difficult when it means changing our habits, such as riding our bikes instead of being driven around by car. Sometimes you have to be uncomfortable to protect the climate, such as when you take part in climate demonstrations.

BUT WOULDN'T YOU RATHER BE A LITTLE UNCOMFORTABLE NOW TO SAVE THE FUTURE CLIMATE FOR ALL OF US?

JUST ANOTHER DAY FOR RESCUING THE CLIMATE—WHAT DECISIONS WILL YOU MAKE?

JUMP OUT OF BED AND TURN UP THE HEAT

A Don't turn it up quite so high.

B Just crank it right up and then open the window if you have to.

Lowering the indoor temperature by only 1°C (1.8°F) can save a lot of energy—and money—over time.

TAKE A SHOWER

A Make it superhot and stand there for ages using shower gel from a plastic bottle.

B Take a shorter shower with pleasantly warm water using soap that doesn't come covered in plastic.

Saves energy, avoids plastic waste, and is better for your skin, too.

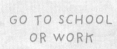

GO TO SCHOOL OR WORK

A Take the car.

B Ride your bike or use public transit if you can.

Prevents or reduces air pollution, and keeps you fit at the same time!

GRAB A SNACK

A Bring a sandwich in a lunch box and a drink in a reusable stainless-steel thermos.

B Eat a sandwich wrapped in plastic, plus drink soda from a can.

IT'S GOOD FOR THE ENVIRONMENT AND LOOKS COOL, TOO!

Not only avoids waste, but also the large amount of energy required to produce disposable packaging.

AT SCHOOL

A Think about how your school can become more climate-friendly, such as in the school cafeteria, or how the topic of the Arctic and climate protection could be brought into the classroom.

B Throw paper airplanes at the teacher.

IT'S MORE FUN AND WILL BE TO YOUR CREDIT, TOO.

Don't leave everything up to the teachers. You can take the initiative yourself. In some places there are even prizes for being the most climate-friendly school!

AFTER LUNCH

A Throw away all the leftover food.

B Keep the leftovers and make something delicious from them the next day.

About one-third of the food that is produced to feed us each year ends up being wasted or lost. This is also contributing to global warming. After all, food production requires land, raw materials, water, and fuel for transport. Throwing away less means having to produce less. That protects the climate, the environment, and your wallet.

GOING SHOPPING

A Let yourself be tempted by every sales pitch.

B Ask yourself whether you really need that new cell phone, shirt, or pair of sneakers.

Raw materials and energy are required at every stage to produce and transport consumer goods. There is often additional environmental damage, for instance, when dyeing new clothes or when valuable raw materials are extracted to make our cell phones and computers.

LUNCHTIME: TO GO WITH SOME CRISPY FRIES

A Enjoy a veggie burger ("plant-based meat" is now made with peas, wheat, etc.).

B Grab a beef burger.

To produce beef, you need pasture and arable land to grow fodder to feed the cows. The animals themselves also produce methane, a greenhouse gas. To calculate the climate impact of the greenhouse gases that are created, there is a unit of measurement called "CO_2 equivalent." Just 1 kilogram (2.2 pounds) of beef produces the equivalent of between 12 and 100 kilograms (between 26.5 and 220.5 pounds) of climate-damaging CO_2. Vegetable alternatives such as protein-rich beans produce on average 2 kilograms (4.4 pounds) of CO_2 equivalents. So if you prefer to eat alternatives to meat, cheese, and milk, you will be protecting the climate.

A GREAT COMPROMISE? BUY SECONDHAND. YOU'LL HAVE SOMETHING NEW TO YOU WITHOUT CAUSING ANY ADDITIONAL DAMAGE, AND YOU'LL HANG ON TO MORE OF YOUR SPENDING MONEY.

AT THE GROCERY STORE

A Depending on the season, try to eat produce grown by local farmers and sold without plastic packaging. Take your own shopping bag to the store.

B Buy food wherever you want, from anywhere around the world. Make sure it's wrapped in plastic and carry it all home in a bag provided by the shop.

Why would you buy strawberries grown in a greenhouse overseas in the middle of winter? It costs a lot of energy to grow and transport them, and they don't even taste good!

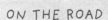
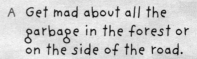

ON THE ROAD

A Get mad about all the garbage in the forest or on the side of the road.

B Get together with a few friends and pick up the litter (wear gloves for this).

Does that sound unfair, when it was someone else who threw the trash away? Maybe so, but it benefits all of us. Post about it online—you'll be sure to get a lot of likes and imitators.

HANGING OUT

A Stream your favorite series in high definition on the biggest screen possible.

B Read a great book.

Streaming movies is fun, but it also uses a lot of energy, especially when streamed via mobile network. Better to watch something via Wi-Fi, on a smaller screen, and at a lower streaming quality. If you just want to listen to music, you can stream the audio only. Streaming music videos that you don't even watch uses unnecessary energy.

ON/OFF

AT NIGHT

A Switch off any unused devices completely.

B Leave the television, computer, and monitor in standby/sleep mode.

Standby is an unnecessary power hog.

DINNER WITH FRIENDS OR FAMILY

A Plan a trip by bike or train.

B Plan your next flight (or even a cruise to the Arctic).

There is no more climate-damaging way to travel than flying. The carbon dioxide emitted from one round-trip flight from New York to London totals about 640 kilograms (about 1,400 pounds) per passenger, according to the UN's ICAO Carbon Emissions Calculator—that's more than the average citizen of Kenya (and more than thirty other countries) emits over a full year. What's worse, CO_2 is only half the problem.

SPEND THE EVENING NAGGING YOUR PARENTS

A To buy you that smartphone that you really, really need.

B To convince them to finally switch to using green electricity.

SAVE THE POLES! GET RID OF COAL!

In 2018, electricity generated by burning coal was responsible for 30 percent of global CO_2 emissions.

113

NOT GOODBYE FOREVER

WOULD YOU LIKE TO HELP PROTECT THE CLIMATE?

The *Polarstern* has traveled with the Arctic sea ice for a year. The people on board have had many adventures. They have encountered polar bears and braved Arctic storms. They have observed life in the dark polar night and studied the interplay of ocean, sea ice, and atmosphere. When the researchers finally bring down the tents and huts, they're looking forward to going home—and yet they're a little sad at the same time. They're finally saying goodbye to an ice world that may well disappear. But it doesn't have to be a goodbye forever. The future of the Arctic is closely linked to our own. We can have a say in what kind of world we want to live in. We can stand up for our future.

THINK THEY'RE NOT INTERESTED? ARE YOU KIDDING? POLITICIANS KNOW VERY WELL THAT YOU WILL SOON BE ABLE TO VOTE.

NOW'S THE TIME

Maybe, like so many young people around the world, you're already working together with other climate protectors and Arctic rescuers. If not, have you ever thought about joining a climate action group? It's never too late to start...

Maybe you want to make some noise and ask politicians to take climate protection seriously.

Maybe you're bravely shaking off the habits that have brought the Earth to the point where even the North Pole is melting. You can educate others (most of them would be grateful for your help) and even come up with new ideas to defend the world against climate change.

Maybe you don't manage to fight for the Arctic and protecting the climate every day. That's okay. You don't have to save the world every minute, and you can't do the right thing all the time. But we should at least try as best we can.

LOOKING TO THE FUTURE

Maybe you've already got big plans for your life.

Maybe you're already planning to do volunteer work for environmental and climate protection or to join a climate club at school.

Maybe you have your eye on a career that will help keep the natural world in balance without using up all of our natural resources. Perhaps you'll even become an innovator or inventor.

Maybe you'll go into politics to help make sure governments make the right decisions.

Maybe you'll start your own climate campaign. Some of the most powerful initiatives have been started by young people.

Maybe you'll even decide to become a polar researcher or a climate scientist. Or a radio operator, photographer, captain, doctor, or meteorologist who works on a research vessel like the *Polarstern* to better understand and protect the natural world.

Maybe we'll see you on one of our next expeditions to the Arctic—an Arctic with sea ice, since we'll have taken such good care of our climate in the meantime.

YOU CAN HELP SHAPE THE FUTURE—FOR THE ARCTIC, AND FOR THE PLANET. IT'S GREAT TO HAVE YOU ON BOARD!

GLOSSARY

AEROSOLS

These are tiny solid particles or liquid droplets in the Earth's atmosphere. They drift around and can be blown over long distances. Many of them have natural sources: they can consist of volcanic ash, pollen, sea salt, desert sand, soot, or even bacteria. There are also anthropogenic aerosols such as smoke. Aerosols are tiny, and yet they have a huge impact on our health (we inhale them with every breath) as well as on our climate. Many of these aerosols work as the nuclei of clouds.

ALBEDO

Albedo is the measure of how strongly the sun's rays are reflected by surfaces such as sea ice, snow, and glacier ice, but also asphalt, forests, and water. The surface properties determine how high the albedo number is. An albedo of 1 means that the radiation is completely reflected. An albedo of 0, on the other hand, means the radiation is completely absorbed. Freshly fallen snow, which is especially bright, has an albedo of up to 0.95. Ice covering a surface of water does not reflect the sun as strongly and so has an albedo of 0.7. Water, on the other hand, reflects barely any radiation and only has an albedo of 0.07 to 0.1, depending on the angle of the sun's rays. Instead of reflecting radiation, it absorbs the sun's rays and warms up as a result.

ALFRED WEGENER INSTITUTE

One of the most famous polar and marine research centers in the world, this institute led the *Polarstern* expedition. Its headquarters is located in Bremerhaven, but it also has research centers in Potsdam and on the islands of Helgoland and Sylt. On the research icebreaker *Polarstern* and other research vessels, institute scientists travel to the most remote regions of the world. They also conduct research at stations such as Neumayer III in Antarctica. The scientists of the Alfred Wegener Institute study how the seas and polar regions of the world are being affected by climate change, and how this is, in turn, affecting the Earth's climate system.

ANTHROPOGENIC

We often talk about the anthropogenic greenhouse effect when we refer to the greenhouse effect and climate change caused by humans. "Anthropogenic" comes from the Greek word *anthropos* ("man") and *gen* ("to arise"). As a technical term, it describes everything that humans have influenced, caused, or manufactured, from materials such as plastic (only humans can produce plastic) to environmental and climate change.

ARCTIC

The region around the North Pole. The opposite region, around the South Pole, is the Antarctic. You can sometimes tell them apart in photographs if you see a polar bear or a penguin. Polar bears exist only in the Arctic, penguins only in the Antarctic. (If they both appear in the same photo, then something is wrong!) The polar cap is in the center of the Arctic. Around it extends the Arctic Ocean. This region, also called the Central Arctic or High Arctic, is one of the most extreme and hostile to life on the planet. But the northern areas of the continents of Asia, Europe, and North America are also part of the Arctic, which includes the eight "Arctic States" of Denmark (Greenland), Finland, Iceland, Canada, Norway (including Svalbard), Russia (Siberia), Sweden, and the USA (Alaska).

ARCTIC OCEAN

Covering 14 million square kilometers (5.4 million square miles), the Arctic Ocean is the smallest ocean in the world. It extends around the North Pole to the adjacent continents. The ocean is losing more and more of its sea ice due to climate change.

ATMOSPHERE

The shell of gases that surrounds the Earth. Without the atmosphere there would be no life on our planet, because the atmosphere ensures a life-friendly temperature and stores the oxygen we need to breathe. This is where our weather happens (and by extension, our climate, which is the average weather over the long term). Climate researchers are interested in everything that happens or is created in the atmosphere, such as clouds, aerosols, winds, turbulence, greenhouse gases, and the ozone layer.

CARBON DIOXIDE / CO_2

This is the main greenhouse and climate gas. The colorless and odorless gas is made up of carbon (C) and oxygen (O). It is a natural part of the Earth's atmosphere and is important to the natural greenhouse effect that makes the planet capable of supporting life. Humans emit carbon dioxide every time we exhale. However, we overdid it with our excessive use of fossil fuels, and as a result the amount of CO_2 in the atmosphere has grown—along with other greenhouse gases—causing global warming. In addition, we have cut down vast areas of forest to create agricultural land, and trees are good absorbers of carbon. CO_2 concentration is measured in parts per million (ppm). Measurements of ancient ice cores have shown that over the past 800,000 years, concentrations have never exceeded 300 ppm. Around 1750, at the beginning of the industrial revolution, it was around 278 ppm. And today? The measurement has exceeded 407 ppm.

CLIMATE

Weather refers to what comes out of the sky over the short term, such as periods of rain or snow, or heat from the sun. Weather changes by the day and sometimes even faster than that. Climate refers to weather that occurs over a long period of time—thirty years or more—and often refers to how the entire climate system works.

CLIMATE CHANGE

Where there's an atmosphere, there has always been climate change. Over long periods of time, the Earth has warmed and cooled, causing ice ages and warming periods, and the climate history of Earth has seen many of them. The difference today is that this change is happening with unprecedented speed, and humans themselves are responsible. The consequences of this change will continue to be felt. Because climate change is getting stronger and having a drastic ecological and social impact on the planet, many are calling it a climate crisis.

CLIMATE MODEL

A climate model is created by a supersmart computer program and offers a kind of forecast for how the climate will develop. To do this modeling, you have to feed these computer programs with data. The accuracy of the forecasts therefore depends on how much good and accurate data the computer program has received.

CLIMATE PROTECTION

The climate changes that have taken place so far cannot be reversed. But it is possible to slow down further climate change and to limit its impact on the Earth and on humans. It's important for individuals, groups, and countries to take action to protect the climate. Many of these measures aim to prevent the Earth from warming by 2°C (3.6°F) or, even better, to keep the warming to 1.5°C (2.7°F). Climate change is one of the greatest challenges facing humanity, but if we all work together, we can prevent the more severe and more dangerous effects. You can find out in part 3 of this book what you can do yourself. Many other tips are available from organizations such as Kids Against Climate Change, NASA's Climate Kids, Greenpeace, and many others.

CLIMATE SYSTEM

The Earth's climate system, sometimes simply referred to as "the climate," is extremely complex. Two very important parts of the climate system are the atmosphere and the cryosphere, the latter being all the frozen areas on the planet. The different parts of the climate system all interact and then change as a result of these interactions. So changes to one part of the system, such as the sea ice, which is part of the cryosphere, will influence other parts, such as the atmosphere.

CRYOSPHERE

This includes all the frozen areas of the planet, such as glaciers, sea ice, and permafrost—soil that remains frozen year-round. The cryosphere is an extremely important part of the global climate system and helps prevent the Earth from excessive warming. Ice and snow have a high albedo and reflect the sun's rays instead of absorbing them and heating up as darker soil would do.

ECOSYSTEM

This includes a living space and the animal and plant species within it. You could say an ecosystem is like a house that is shared by many different inhabitants, in which everything is connected and everyone depends on each other (the word comes from the Greek *oikos* for "house" and *systema* for "connected"). Changes to different parts of this shared space can put the whole house in danger.

EXPEDITION

According to its Latin roots, the word "expedition" originally referred to journeys undertaken for settlement, or military campaigns such as those led by Caesar. But this original meaning has been lost. Today "expedition" mostly refers to scientific research explorations that present major logistical and planning challenges in remote areas.

EXTREME WEATHER

Storms, heavy rains, droughts, and cold fronts can all be referred to as extreme weather events when they are unusual in a certain season for a certain place. Although no single extreme weather event can be attributed to anthropogenic climate change, more extreme weather events are happening more often.

FOSSIL FUELS

Humans use these as our preferred energy source, but they are also the cause of climate change. They include carbon-based fuels such as coal, oil, natural gas, or even peat. When these fuels are burned, they produce carbon dioxide, or CO_2. Since the beginning of the industrial age, fossil fuels have been used in such large amounts that the concentrations of carbon dioxide in the Earth's atmosphere have increased by almost 50 percent. Fortunately, however, people are working to slow down this increase: there are now many alternative energy sources, such as renewable energy like wind and solar power. Other technologies are being developed, like hydrogen-fueled cars. We are also coming up with smarter ways to get people from place to place, such as efficient public transportation, and using bicycles, electric cars, and ride-sharing, where people share cars and use them only when truly needed.

FRAM EXPEDITION

In 1893–1896, Fridtjof Nansen became the first researcher to venture across the Arctic by letting his expedition ship, *Fram*, drift with the natural movement of the sea ice. Although the *Fram* did not achieve its goal of reaching the geographical North Pole, this was one of the greatest expeditions in the history of polar research. Today the ship sits in a museum in Oslo, Norway.

FUTURE

The future is not just a distant time that may or may not affect us at some point. The future is instead directly related to the present. We can influence it now and thus have a say in what kind of world we or our children will live in. We have huge power over the future, and we can shape it if we decide to.

GREENHOUSE EFFECT

In a garden greenhouse, the sun shines through the glass roof to warm the air and earth inside the house. The glass prevents the heated air from leaving the house again, so the inside stays nice and warm. The greenhouse effect of our planet works in a very similar way. The sun's rays hit the surface of the Earth. The surface then emits thermal radiation—heat. But instead of a glass roof, it is greenhouse gases in the atmosphere that hold in this thermal radiation and warm the planet. Without this natural greenhouse effect the Earth would be an icy ball. But now people are causing more and more greenhouse gases to be released into the atmosphere, creating more warmth and causing the Earth's temperatures to rise. So a human-made greenhouse effect is being added to the natural one. The result is climate change.

GREENHOUSE GAS

Gases in the atmosphere cause the natural greenhouse effect and the anthropogenic (human-origin) greenhouse effect. The most important greenhouse gases are water vapor (H_2O), carbon dioxide (CO_2), nitrous oxide (N_2O), methane (CH_4), and ozone (O_3).

ICE DRIFT

Sea ice does not stay in the same place on the water. Wind and ocean currents cause it to drift across the ocean in certain directions. There are two major drift movements in the Arctic: the transpolar drift goes from the Siberian coast toward the Fram Strait, which runs between Greenland and Spitsbergen, and the Beaufort Gyre is a gigantic vortex above the north coasts of Alaska, Greenland, and Canada.

INDUSTRIAL AGE / INDUSTRIAL REVOLUTION

From the second half of the eighteenth century, after the invention of the steam engine, a period of rapid industrial growth that started in the United Kingdom began to change the world. Factories emerged, goods and commodities were produced in ever larger quantities, and cities grew. Society itself changed as many new things were made for the benefit of humans. At the same time, more and more fossil fuels were burned, creating a greater output of greenhouse gases, especially carbon dioxide.

MOSAiC EXPEDITION

Scientific enterprises often have strange abbreviations for long complicated names. The 2019–2020 *Polarstern* expedition, the largest Arctic expedition in history, is called MOSAiC, which stands for Multidisciplinary drifting Observatory for the Study of Arctic Climate. The name represents many different scientific disciplines working together to explore the Arctic climate system. Directed by the Alfred Wegener Institute in Germany, more than eighty research institutes from twenty nations are involved in this mammoth expedition. But the name is also fitting because the research camp of the MOSAiC expedition stood on an ice floe that kept cracking and sometimes truly looked like a mosaic.

PERMAFROST

This is soil that remains constantly frozen and is found in places such as northern Canada or high in the Alps. But global warming is causing these soils to thaw, creating a so-called tipping point that worries many scientists. This means that just a tiny change can tip a situation into one with serious and irreversible consequences. If enough permafrost thaws, strong greenhouse gases will be released from the soil, adding to those already in the atmosphere and accelerating global warming.

PLANKTON

These tiny living things float freely in water (in ancient Greek the word means "errant" or "the wandering"). Science distinguishes between phytoplankton (plant plankton) and zooplankton (animal plankton), which includes supertiny crustaceans and snails.

POLAR 5 AND POLAR 6

These two colorful research aircraft of the Alfred Wegener Institute can withstand the extreme environmental conditions of the polar regions and fly in temperatures as low as -54°C (-65°F). Other planes would have been unable to fly through the air to get there, let alone able to start and land. These robust aircraft were used by the Allies back in World War II but have been updated with state-of-the-art technology. They can even be equipped with skis so they can land on snow. They have instruments on board to investigate the atmosphere and sea ice.

SEA ICE

Sea ice floats on the ocean and forms when seawater freezes beneath a cold atmosphere. Since sea ice melts in summer and the seawater refreezes in winter, its extent and thickness change over the years and seasons.

ACKNOWLEDGMENTS

This book has been made possible through the support of many people. The author especially thanks AWI directors Antje Boetius, Karsten Wurr, Uwe Nixdorf, and expedition leader Markus Rex for the opportunity to accompany the MOSAiC expedition. Thanks to Dorothea Bauch, Boris Christian, Jessie Creamean, Ying-Chih Fang, Hauke Flores, Rolf Gradinger, Klaus Grosfeld, Christian Haas, Clara Hoppe, Mario Hoppmann, Sybille Klenzendorf, Boris Koch, Bjela König, Thomas Krumpen, Sina Löschke, Katja Metfies, Roland Neuber, Marcel Nicolaus, Ilka Peeken, Hans-Otto Pörtner, Volker Rachold, Christian Salewski, Ingo Sasgen, Janin Schaffer, Julia Schmale, Kirstin Schulz, and Anja Sommerfeld for consulting on the content of this book, and everyone else who shared their expertise and photographs. Special thanks also go to Stefanie Arndt, Lisa Grosfeld, Sebastian Grote, Esther Horvath, and Folke Mehrtens for their support and access to the official logbook entries from on board the *Polarstern*, and to Annika Meyer/eventfive and the team from meereisportal.de for help with the graphics. Many thanks go to Anette Weiß and Stephanie Roderer for their patient and careful work with editing and layout. And another thank-you goes out to Shelley Tanaka, Linda Pruessen, Chandra Wohleber, Alison Strobel, Stephen Ullstrom, and Jessica Sullivan for their fabulous work on the English edition of the book. And we particularly thank our families, who have given us so much support during our trips to the Arctic and our continued work on this book. The author would especially like to thank her husband, Jens Tuider, whose advice guided her through this book project as confidently as the icebreaker *Polarstern* led the expedition through the sea ice.

KATHARINA WEISS-TUIDER and
CHRISTIAN SCHNEIDER

PHOTO CREDITS

INDEX

Note: Illustrations and photographs are indicated by page numbers in **bold**

© Hans Honold

AUTHOR

KATHARINA WEISS-TUIDER accompanied the MOSAIC expedition as communications manager at the Alfred Wegener Institute. As a participant in the expedition, she was able to explore the Arctic and experience its changes for herself. She has a doctorate in literary studies from LMU Munich and has had a long career as a freelance author, writing about the environment, climate, food, and agriculture. She lives in Berlin with her husband, with whom she works to protect the climate, environment, and animals. The protection of the Arctic has been especially important to her ever since she saw her first polar bear in the wild.

© privat

ILLUSTRATOR

CHRISTIAN SCHNEIDER was born in Darmstadt and studied illustration in Hamburg. He loves nature in all its facets, which he captures on paper with colored pencil. He especially enjoys glimpses of the foxes that live in his neighborhood—a touch of wilderness in the urban jungle of Berlin.

© Samay Claro

GRAPHIC DESIGNER

STEPHANIE RODERER was born in Munich and studied new media and design in Austria before establishing her own design company. She loves hiking in the outdoors, which is where she gets her best ideas. When she's not in the mountains, you'll probably find her in her Munich studio, where she polishes and shapes those ideas.

First published in English by Greystone Books in 2023
Originally published in German in 2021 as *Expedition Polarstern: Dem Klimawandel auf der Spur* by Katharina Weiss-Tuider © 2021 by cbj Verlag, a division of Penguin Random House Verlagsgruppe GmbH, München, Germany
Translation copyright © 2023 by Shelley Tanaka

23 24 25 26 27   5 4 3 2 1

Greystone Kids / Greystone Books Ltd.
greystonebooks.com

Cataloguing data available from Library and Archives Canada
ISBN 978-1-77164-956-8 (cloth)
ISBN 978-1-77164-957-5 (epub)

Editing by Linda Pruessen
Copy editing by Chandra Wohleber
Proofreading by Alison Strobel
Indexing by Stephen Ullstrom
German edition design by Stephanie Roderer
English edition cover design by Jessica Sullivan
Cover illustrations by Christian Schneider

Printed and bound in Malaysia on FSC® certified paper at Imago Group. The FSC® label means that this product is made of material from well-managed FSC®-certified forests, recycled materials, and other controlled sources.

Greystone Books thanks the Canada Council for the Arts, the British Columbia Arts Council, the Province of British Columbia through the Book Publishing Tax Credit, and the Government of Canada for supporting our publishing activities.

The translation of this work was supported by a grant from the Goethe-Institut.

Greystone Books gratefully acknowledges the xʷməθkʷəy̓əm (Musqueam), Sḵwx̱wú7mesh (Squamish), and səl̓ílwətaɬ (Tsleil-Waututh) peoples on whose land our Vancouver head office is located.